simple knits for little cherubs

erika knight

simple knits for little cherubs

photography by john heseltine

COLLINS & BROWN

First published in Great Britain in 2003 by
Collins & Brown
64 Brewery Road
N7 9NT

A member of Chrysalis Books plc

This book was conceived and produced by Susan Berry for
Collins & Brown Ltd.

Technical Editor: Eva Yates
Designer: Debbie Mole
Styling: Erika Knight & Susan Berry

British Library Cataloguing-in-Publication Data: A catalogue record
for this book is available from the British Library

ISBN: 1 84340 018 9

Reproduction by: Classican, Singapore
Printed by: Kyodo Printing Co (S'Pore) Pte Ltd

1 3 5 7 9 10 8 6 4 2

contents: introduction **7** • yarns and colours **8** • equipment & tension **10** • sizing **12** • classic sweater **18** • short-sleeved sweater **24** • denim pinafore **30** • girl's games sweater **36** • fluffy bolero **42** • dressing gown **46** • scottie dog cardigan **56** • fairisle border cardigan **62** • boy's diamond pullover **68** • reindeer zipper cardigan **74** • stripy hat **82** • stripy muffler **86** • mittens on strings **90** • simple socks **94** • patched blanket **98** • velvet rabbit **102** • pyjama bag **106** • top dog **110** • erika's tips **118** • substituting yarns **121** • suppliers **123** • acknowledgements **128** •

introduction

THIS IS A COLLECTION of *classic vintage knits* for little children aged *two to five years*; retro in feel, it offers a nostalgic look at the values of childhood, like *snapshots through a family album,* which are both evocative and treasured. It celebrates that beautiful age when a child is utterly absorbed with a stick, a puddle or a stone on the beach, and when their little legs are small enough to stick out straight in front of them when they are seated on a chair!

The palette is *unashamedly retro;* muted soft tones of oatmeal and charcoal marls, old rose pinks and lavender blues with bolder statements of black and white. The photography captures the charm of childhood with close-up shots, children playing together or absorbed in a single pursuit of their own making: building bricks, a cardboard box, making a camp, taking tea with teddy friends, and dressing in their own unique way when left to choose for themselves!

The yarns come in three weights: fine, medium and chunky, to make sourcing and selection much easier. The patterns introduce *simple techniques and details* that provide a classic timeless quality, with a touch of personalization in simple Fairisle borders, little motifs, pockets and trims.

It is always great fun to knit for little children, the pieces are small and manageable, and children always seem to be in need of something new, as they grow so very quickly. With this in mind this book aims to inspire a new generation of hand-me downs; unashamedly nostalgic in concept, yet elegantly restrained and modern in approach. I hope you will find a favourite among the designs, to be knitted time and time again, to create heirlooms to treasure long after the little cherubs have grown and flown, which one day they might return to for their own children.

erika knight

yarns and colours

YARNS: I choose to use natural fibres, which allow the skin to breathe. They absorb moisture, keeping the body cool in summer and warm in winter, and thus remain ultimately comfortable; an important quality when knitting for little children. I have selected fine merino wools, soft cottons, and blends of both to wear all year round, which combine the warmth and elasticity of wool with the excellent cool properties and drape of cotton. I can never resist, however, the ultimate luxury of beautiful yarns such as mohair, silk, chenille and cashmere. They wash and wear extremely well.

If your child has allergies, cotton is a good substitute for wool, and most of the patterns can be substituted with cotton. Alternatively, look for cotton microfibres, which boast technological refinement with all the comfort of natural products. If you are taking the time to knit for your own enjoyment or for someone a little special, use the very best materials, value your work and the time spent as worthwhile, to make it a joy!

right: Fine, medium and chunky-weight yarns in merino wool, cotton and luxury blends give a different characteristic to classic styles, to knit time and time again.

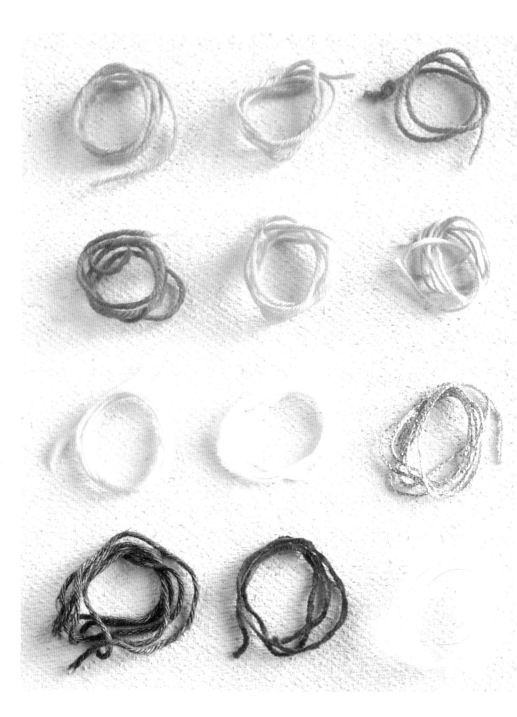

COLOURS: I have opted for a deliberately retro palette, in which soft muted tones predominate as opposed to the usual bright colours chosen for children.

I have selected classic neutrals as a base, in a mélange: that is, mixed with another tone to create a soft, slightly textured base, in oatmeal and flannel grey, which are ideal for combining with Fairisle patterns. The latter work extreme-ly well, too, with tints and hints of chalky or lavender blue, rose pinks and warm greys.

Brighter highlights of raspberry, spruce and indigo add interest to some patterns, and in one pattern black and ecru (as opposed to white) make a striking impact in an unashamedly retro design.

All the colours harmonize so if you want to use up yarns for projects such as the scarf, hat, socks or blanket, you will find you can easily do this by buying just a couple of extra balls, making the garments economical as well as attractive – always a consideration with children's clothes.

left: Natural yarns take colour beautifully. The soft, compatible palette shown here is perfect for retro styles. Look for interesting trims to personalize your knits – grosgrain, silk and gingham ribbons or mother-of-pearl, bone or vintage buttons.

equipment and tension

The equipment for knitting is simple and readily available. It consists principally of the needles and the yarn. The yarn qualities have been discussed on the previous page, but the combination of needle size with yarn weight will determine the stitch size (known as tension) and the eventual garment size.

NEEDLES: For the designs featured in this book you will require the following size needles 2.75mm (US 1), 3mm (US 2), 3.25mm (US 3), 3.75mm (US 5), 4mm (US 6), 4.5mm (US 7) and 6.5mm (US $10^1/2$).

I prefer to use bamboo needles, which are naturally smooth and light, and silent! They make knitting a real pleasure. If working the lengths of rouleau for the mittens, dressing gown or pymama bag, you will also need a pair of double-pointed needles. And the odd spare needle is useful on which to leave stitches, as required by the pattern.

SCISSORS: These are required for cutting yarns and loose ends on the knitting. You will also use them if making pompoms for the velvet rabbit project or the pyjama bag.

SEWING NEEDLE: A large blunt-ended sewing needle is required to sew up the knitting, generally with the yarn from the project, unless otherwise stated.

TAPE MEASURE: You will need a tape measure for taking your child's measurements, checking your tension and measuring the knitting as you work. Make sure the tape measure is accurate and not stretched, through constant use.

PINS: You will need some pins to mark your tension square, to mark intervals in your knitting for picking up stitches or for holding pieces of the knitted fabric together while you sew them up. Safety pins are useful too for keeping stitches on that will be picked up and worked on later for necklines, for example.

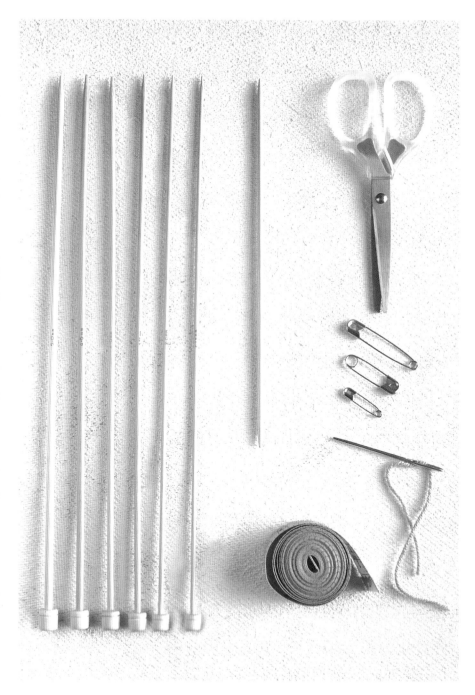

TENSION: I love the actual process of knitting; the making of the loop, then a series of loops and stitches, and then the rows of stitches until at last I have created a textile, which I can design in a variety of ways and for a variety of purposes. There are very few rules – I hate to have rules – but if there is one to be mastered that will help you produce great knitting it is that of tension (also known as gauge or stitch size). Tension simply refers to the number of stitches and number of rows to each square inch or centimetre of knitted fabric. It should be even and maintained throughout the work. The actual tension required for each garment or pattern in this book is always specified at the beginning of each pattern, in the paragraph marked 'stitch size'.

If you take time at the beginning to ensure that the tension of your knitting is the same as that of the pattern, it saves time in the end. It ensures the finished project exactly duplicates the given pattern, avoding disappointment.

To check your tension, make a sample at least 15cm (6in) square, using the yarn, needle size and stitch given in the stitch size instruction at the start of each pattern. Lay the work out on a flat smooth surface, taking care not to stretch it. With a ruler or tape measure, mark out a square 10cm (4in) with pins. Then count the number of stitches between the pins.

If the number of stitches and rows does not correspond with the tension stated in the pattern, you need to change needle size. If the number of stitches and rows is less than stated, your tension is too loose. Try again on a finer needle or your finished project will be too big. If the number of stitches and rows is more than stated, try again on larger needles, or your finished project will be too small.

Continue to try different needle sizes until the number of stitches and rows is the same as stated in the pattern.

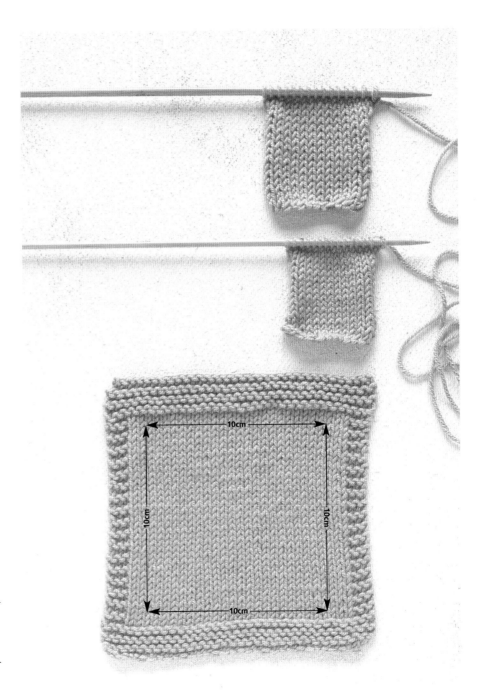

sizing: how to measure your child

right: Take time to measure your child properly before you start to knit. The measurements shown on the doll, right, indicate the key measurements you need to take. Once you have measured your child, use the size gradings shown overleaf to determine which sizing in the pattern to choose. The most important measurement to start with is chest width: the body length of the garment, or the sleeve length, can be easily adjusted.

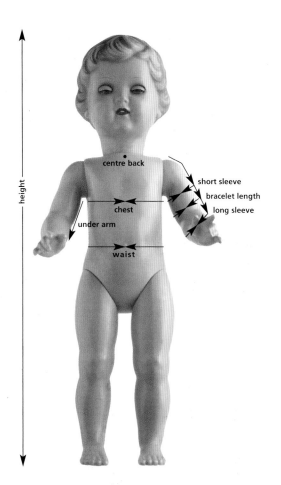

in the chest measurement (for room to move), and there is generally a 2.5cm (1in) difference in the length between the sizes. I prefer to go by these measurements and by the height, rather than by the age of the child. Length measurements are given for each design. Should you wish to adjust the length, you can add or subtract rows before you start to shape at the armhole.

MEASURING YOUR CHILD

HEIGHT: measure without shoes, with the feet together, from the top of the head to the floor.

CHEST: measure around the fullest part of the chest, close under the arms.

LENGTH: measure from the centre back neck to the natural waistline.

WAIST: measure around the natural waistline.

SLEEVE LENGTH: measure from the centre back neck to the wrist for a long sleeve. From the centre back neck to 10cm (4in) from the wrist for a bracelet or three-quarter length sleeve, and from the centre back neck to the fullest part of the arm for a short sleeve.

Measure from under the arm to the wrist for extra detail.

The projects are designed to fit little children from approximately two years to five years of age, with room for growth. Each pattern comes in three sizes, roughly for a 2 to 3 year old, 3 to 4 year old and 4 to 5 year old.

The sizing guide overleaf gives both a chest size and a length measurement for each garment. The amount of ease has been calculated for each individual design to create a particular look and may vary from pattern to pattern; many of the designs are a little closer fitting in keeping with current trends. The measurements allow 5cm (2in) of ease

SAFETY: It is very important when making anything for little children to keep safety in mind. Toys especially should be sewn securely and must not feature any trim which could work loose, hence felt is used as a simple but effective trim to create character and keep practicality in mind. Wherever possible, toys are designed to avoid lots of little pieces which have to sewn on separately. Use washable stuffing which conforms to safety standards and take extreme care to check for any pins or needles which may have been used in making up.

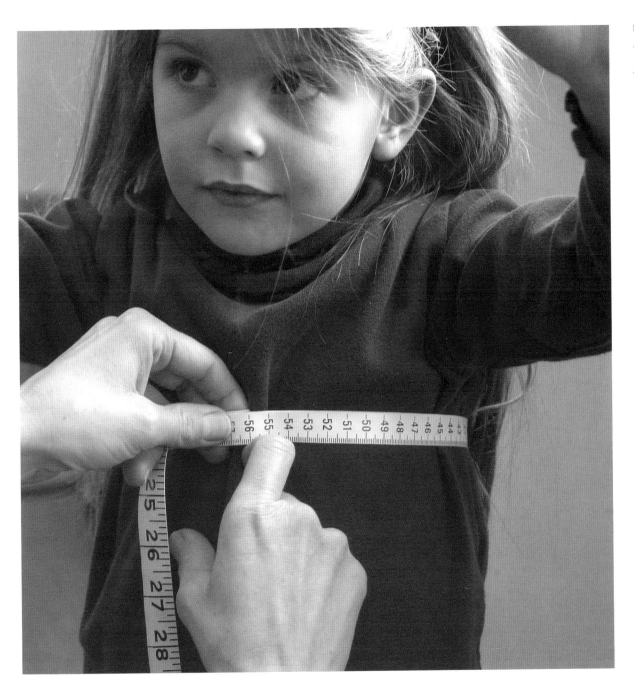

left: Measure your child around the fullest part of the chest, just under the arms. The amount of 'ease' has already been calculated for each pattern, so match your measurements to the sizings given overleaf for each garment.

sizing: for garments

The trend has been for oversized knitted garments for children for quite some time, with drop shoulders and tunic-style shapes. The designs featured in this book unashamedly look back at vintage styling, when children were dressed as children. The shapes are slightly closer fitting yet never tight, allowing for layering and comfort.

The measurements for the patterns in this book are given in three sizes, approximately to fit children aged 2-3, 3-4 and 4-5. A master size chart is given below to check average heights and chest; lengths and widths have been calculated in the design of the garment to give comfort and room for growth without sacrificing style, especially when grading to the larger sizes, which can often be disproportionate in knitting patterns.

Make sure you measure your child first, using the information on the previous page, and then choose the pattern size that most closely corresponds. Your two year old may well be the size of an average three year old for example!

classic sweater

LENGTH (IN/CM)	12 14 16	30.5 36 40
CHEST (IN/CM)	22 24 26	56 61 66
FLAT WIDTH (IN/CM)	11 12 13	23 30.5 33
SLEEVE LENGTH UNDERARM (IN/CM)	8 10 11	21.5 25.5 29

short-sleeved sweater

LENGTH (IN/CM)	13 14 15	33 36 38
CHEST (IN/CM)	22 24 26	56 61 66
FLAT WIDTH (IN/CM)	11 12 13	28 30.5 33
SLEEVE LENGTH UNDERARM (IN/CM)	2 3 3	6 7.5 9

master size chart

AGE:	(YEARS)	2-3	3-4	4-5
HEIGHT:	(CM)	84-91	91-99	99-107
	(IN)	33-36	36-39	39-42
ALL AROUND	(CM)	53-56	56-58	58.5-61
CHEST:	(IN)	21-22	22-23	23-24
FLAT BODY	(CM)	31	33	36
WIDTH:	(IN)	12	13	14
LENGTH FROM	(CM)	32	33	36
CENTRE BACK:	(IN)	12.5	13	14
SLEEVE LENGTH	(CM)	24	27	30
UNDERARM	(IN)	9.5	10.5	12

denim pinafore

LENGTH (IN/CM)	22 23 24	56 58.5 61
CHEST (IN/CM)	21 22 23	53 56 59
FLAT WIDTH (IN/CM)	10 11 11	26.5 28 29.5
SLEEVE LENGTH UNDERARM (IN/CM)	-	-

girl's games sweater

LENGTH (IN/CM)	14 15 16	36 38 41
CHEST (IN/CM)	21 22 23	53 56 59
FLAT WIDTH (IN/CM)	10 11 11	26.5 28 29.5
SLEEVE LENGTH UNDERARM (IN/CM)	7 8 9	18 20 23

fluffy bolero

LENGTH (IN/CM)	9 10 11	23 25.5 28
CHEST (IN/CM)	25 27 29	64 68 74
FLAT WIDTH (IN/CM)	12 13 14	32 34 37
SLEEVE LENGTH UNDERARM (IN/CM)	4 4 5	10.5 12 14

boys diamond pullover

LENGTH (IN/CM)	13 14 15	33 36 38
CHEST (IN/CM)	24 25 26	61 64 66
FLAT WIDTH (IN/CM)	12 12 13	30.5 32 33
ARMHOLE DEPTH (IN/CM)	4 4 5	11 13 14

dressing gown

LENGTH (IN/CM)	22 24 26	56 61 66
CHEST (IN/CM)	27 29 31	34 37 39
FLAT WIDTH (IN/CM)	13 14 15	17 18.5 19.5
SLEEVE LENGTH UNDERARM (IN/CM)	9 10 11	24 27 29

reindeer zipper cardigan

LENGTH (IN/CM)	13 14 15	33 36 38
CHEST (IN/CM)	26 28 30	61 64 66
FLAT WIDTH (IN/CM)	13 14 15	30.5 32 33
SLEEVE LENGTH UNDERARM (IN/CM)	10 11 12	11 13 14

scottie dog cardigan

LENGTH (IN/CM)	12 13 14	32 34 36
CHEST (IN/CM)	24 26 28	61 68 72
FLAT WIDTH (IN/CM)	12 13 14	30.5 34 36
SLEEVE LENGTH UNDERARM (IN/CM)	9 10 11	24 27 30.5

mittens on strings

LENGTH (IN/CM)	5 6	12.5 15
CHEST (IN/CM)	-	-
FLAT WIDTH (IN/CM)	-	-
SLEEVE LENGTH UNDERARM (IN/CM)	-	-

fairisle border cardigan

LENGTH (IN/CM)	13 14 15	34 37 39
CHEST (IN/CM)	22 24 26	56 61 66
FLAT WIDTH (IN/CM)	11 12 13	28 30.5 33
SLEEVE LENGTH UNDERARM (IN/CM)	9 10 12	23 27 30.5

simple socks

LENGTH (IN/CM)	3 4 5	9.5 12 14.5
CHEST (IN/CM)	-	-
FLAT WIDTH (IN/CM)	-	-
SLEEVE LENGTH UNDERARM (IN/CM)	-	-

plain classics

classic sweater

This little sweater is knitted in a medium-weight merino wool and cotton blend, which has all the warmth of wool with the drape of cotton, making it perfect all year round. The pattern offers a choice of a round neck with a buttoned shoulder detail or a V-neck with an integral rib detail, which does not involve picking up stitches and requires less sewing up. If you wish, you can work them with finishing details, like a tip of colour at the base of the rib (see mittens on pages 90-93).

how to make **the classic sweater**

left: A soft wool/cotton blend can be worn next to the skin without discomfort, as many children have very sensitive skin.

right: The V-necked version of this classic pattern slips easily over any child's head. The fully fashioned detailing on the armholes and neck gives it classic appeal

MATERIALS: Medium-weight yarn (DK yarn) eg Rowan wool cotton (50 per cent merino wool/50 per cent cotton) • 4 (5:5) x 50g balls • Pair 3.25mm (US 3) needles • Pair 4 mm (US 6) needles • 3 pearl buttons • Spare needle • Safety pin • Sewing needle.

SWEATER SIZE: For sizing refer to chart on pages 14–15.

STITCH SIZE: This has a stitch size of 22 stitches and 30 rows to 10cm (4in) measured over stocking (stockinette) stitch using using 4mm (US 6) needles.

METHOD: BACK: With 3.25mm (US 3) needles cast on 62 (68:74) stitches. Work in knit 1, purl 1 rib for 4.5 (5:5)cm/ 1³/4 (2:2)in. Change to 4mm (US 6) needles and stocking (stockinette) stitch. Continue until the work measures 18 (21.5:25)cm/7 (8¹/2:10)in ending with a purl row.

SHAPE ARMHOLES: Cast off 4 (4:4) stitches at the beginning of the next 2 rows. Decrease 1 stitch (3 stitches in, see page 118) at each end of the next 6 (6:6) rows. *(42:48:54 stitches)*. Continue without shaping until the work measures 30.5 (35.5:40.5) cm/12 (14:16)in.

SHAPE THE SHOULDERS: Cast off 6 (7:8) stitches at the

left and right: If you sew up the side seams using mattress stitch, in which a stitch is taken from each piece, it produces a neat finish with no bulky seams to cause irritation.

right: The fully fashioned detailing of the armholes and V-neck is shown here in close up. The decreases are worked two stitches in from the end of the row to create a visible feature.

beginning of the next 4 rows. Leave the remaining 18 (20:22) stitches on a spare needle.

FRONT (BOTH VERSIONS): With 3.25mm (US 3) needles, cast on 62 (68:74) stitches. Work in knit 1, purl 1 rib for 4.5 (5:5)cm /1³⁄4 (2:2)in.

Change to 4mm (US 6) needles and stocking (stockinette) stitch, continue until the work measures 18 (21.5:25)cm/7 (8¹⁄2:10)in, ending with a purl row.

SHAPE ARMHOLES: Cast off 4 (4:4) stitches at the beginning of the next 2 rows.

Decrease 1 stitch (3 stitches in, see page 118) at each end of the next 6 (6:6) rows. *(42 48:54 stitches)*

ROUND-NECK BUTTONED-SHOULDER SWEATER: Continue without shaping until the work measures 25.5 (29:33)cm/10 (11¹⁄2:13)in from the beginning, ending with a purl row.

SHAPE NECK: Next row: knit 18 (21:24) stitches. TURN.

Working on these stitches only, continue as follows:

Decrease 1 stitch (3 stitches in) at the neck edge of the next 6 (7:8) rows. *(12:14:16 stitches)*

Continue without shaping until the work measures 28

(33:38)cm/11 (13:15)in from the beginning, ending with a purl row.

Leave the stitches on a stitch holder.

Slip the next 6 stitches onto a safety pin
and with the right side of the work
facing, rejoin the yarn to the neck edge
of the remaining 18 (21:24) stitches and
work as follows:

Next row: knit.

Next rows: decrease 1 stitch (3 stitches
in) at the neck edge on the next 6 (7:8)
rows. *(12:14:16 stitches)*

Continue without shaping until the
work measures 30.5 (35.5:40.5)cm/12
(14:16)in from the beginning, ending
with a knit row.

SHAPE SHOULDER: **Row 1:** cast off 6
(7:8) stitches, purl to the end of the row.

Row 2: knit.

Cast off the remaining 6 (7:8) stitches.
Join the right shoulder seam.

NECKBAND: With the right side facing
and using 3.25mm (US 3) needles, pick
up and knit 14 (16:18) stitches evenly down the left side of
the neck, work across the 6 stitches on the safety pin in knit
1, purl, 1 rib, then pick up and knit 20 (22:24) stitches
evenly up the right side of the neck and finally rib, (starting
with knit 1) across the 18 (20: 22) stitches of the back.
(58:64:70 stitches)

Work in knit 1, purl 1 rib as set for 5 rows.

Cast off in rib.

above: Neat and simple, this
classic sweater has a round
neck with a three-buttoned
shoulder opening. A ribbed
hem, cuffs and neckband
ensure a snug fit.

SHOULDER BUTTONHOLE BAND:
With right side facing and using
3.25mm (US 3) needles, rejoin the yarn
to the stitches left on holder. Knit
across stitches, then pick up 5 stitches
from the edge of the neckband
(17:19:21 stitches)

Row 1: knit 1, purl 1 rib.

Row 2: Make buttonholes. Rib 0 (2:4)
stitches, *rib 3 stitches, yarn round
needle, knit 2 stitches together, repeat
from * twice, rib 2.

Work 2 more rows in rib. Cast off in
rib.

SHOULDER BUTTON BAND: Pick up
and knit 12 (14:16) stitches from the
left back shoulder and 5 stitches from
the neckband. Work 5 rows in stocking
(stockinette) stitch. Purl 1 row. Cast off.

INTEGRAL V-NECK SWEATER: Next row:
knit 21 (24:27) stitches. TURN.

Working on these stitches, continue as
follows:

Rib 5 stitches, purl 2 stitches together, purl to the end of the
row.

Now knit 2 stitches together at the neck edge (inside the
rib border) on the next and every following 4th row to 17
(19:21) stitches.

Now, still working the 5-stitch rib edge, continue without
shaping until the work measures 30.5 (35.5:40.5)cm/12
(14:16) in from the beginning, ending with a purl row.

SHAPE SHOULDER: Cast off 6 (7:8) stitches at the beginning of the next and following alternate row.

Now continue to work the 5 rib stitches for a further 6cm (2^1/4in) to meet the centre back neck. Cast off.

With right side facing, rejoin yarn to the remaining stitches and knit across stitches.

Next row: purl to last 7 stitches, purl 2 stitches together through back loop, rib 5 stitches.

Next row: rib 5 stitches, knit 2 stitches together through back loop, knit to the end.

Now decrease through the back loop (inside the rib border)on every following 4th row to l7 (19:21) stitches.

Continue without shaping until work measures 30.5 (35.5:40.5)cm/12 (14:16) in, ending with knit row.

SHAPE SHOULDER: Cast off 6 (7:8) stitches at the beginning of the next and following alternate row. Continue on the 5 rib stitches for a further 6cm (2^1/4in) to meet the centre back neck. Cast off.

SLEEVES (MAKE TWO THE SAME):
Using 3.25mm (US 3) needles, cast on 36 (38:40) stitches. Work in knit 1, purl 1 rib for 4.5 (5:5) cm /1^3/4 (2:2)in.

Change to 4mm (US 6) needles and stocking

above: Simple and comfortable, this classic sweater is very versatile. The blend of wool and cotton drapes well and is warm in winter, and cool in summer.

(stockinette) stitch.

Increase 1 stitch at both ends of next and every following 6th row until there are 48 (52: 56) stitches.

Continue without shaping until the work measures 21.5 (25:29)cm/8^1/2 (10:11^1/2)in from the beginning.

SHAPE TOP: cast off 4 stitches at the beginning of each of the next 2 rows. Decrease 1 stitch (3 stitches in) at each end of next and following alternate rows until 26 (24:22) stitches remain. Purl 1 row.

Decrease 1 stitch (3 stitches in) at each end of every row until 10 (12:14) stitches remain. Cast off.

MAKE UP: Weave in all the ends. Lay work out flat, and steam gently, avoiding the rib trims.

ROUND-NECK BUTTONED-SHOULDER SWEATER: Place the rib buttonhole band over the buttonband on the left shoulder and sew at the armhole edge. Set the sleeves into the armholes, and sew up with mattress stitch (see page 119). Sew sleeve and side seams with mattress stitch. Sew on buttons to correspond with buttonholes.

INTEGRAL V-NECK SWEATER: Sew shoulder seams. Join the rib neck edges at the centre back with mattress stitch and sew rib edging around the back neck. Set and sew sleeves into the armholes, and sew sleeve and side seams using mattress stitch.

short-sleeved sweater

Simply classic, this little sweater is worked in stocking
(stockinette) stitch with narrow rib trims. It has touches
of fully fashioning detail to make it a piece you will want
to knit time and time again. The short sleeves makes it
ideal for wearing under the Fairisle cardigan (see pages
62-7), or make both plain if you prefer. The neck has a
simple back opening to help it pass easily over the
child's head. Either trim it with a silk ribbon and tie it in
a bow, or sew on a little button to fasten. For a special
touch, embroider it with a flower or make it in lurex or
cashmere for a party piece.

left: The set-in sleeves have a
neat fully fashioned detail,
and are finished just above
the elbow with a narrow band
of knit 1, purl 1 rib.

how to make **the short-sleeved sweater**

MATERIALS: Fine yarn (4 ply yarn) e.g. Jaeger Matchmaker 100 per cent merino wool • 3 (3:4) x 50g balls • Pair 2.75mm (US 1) needles • Pair 3.25mm (US 3) needles • Stitch holder • Sewing needle • Trim and or one very small button

SIZING: For sizing refer to chart on page 14–15.

STITCH SIZE: This sweater has a stitch size of 28 stitches and 36 rows to 10cm (4in) measured over stocking (stockinette) stitch using 3.25mm (US 3) needles.

METHOD: BACK: With 2.75mm (US 1) needles cast on 80 (86:92) stitches. Work 3cm/1^1/4in in knit 1, purl 1 rib. Change to 3.25mm (US 3) needles and stocking (stockinette) stitch. Continue until work measures 21.5 (23:24)cm/8^1/2 (9:9^1/2)in, ending with a purl row.

SHAPE ARMHOLE: cast off 7 (7:7) stitches at beginning of next 2 rows. Then decrease 1 stitch at each end (3 stitches in from edge – see page 118) of next 4 (6:8) rows. *(58 :60:62 stitches)*

Continue without shaping until armhole measures 6.5 (7.5:9)cm/2^1/2 (3:3^1/2)in, ending with a purl row.

MAKE CENTRE BACK NECK SPLIT: Next row: knit 29 (30: 31) stitches, TURN and knitting the 2 stitches at the centre back edge on every row, continue until armhole measures 11.5 (13:14)cm/4^1/2 (5:5^1/2)in from start of armhole shaping, ending at armhole edge.

SHAPE SHOULDER: **Row 1:** cast off 5 (5:6) stitches, knit to end. **Row 2:** purl. **Row 3:** cast off 5 (6:6) stitches, knit to end. **Row 4:** purl. **Row 5:** cast off 6 (6:6) stitches, knit to end. **Row 6:** purl (Shoulder shaping now finished).

opposite: Knitted in fine
merino wool, this versatile
little sweater is a must for
every small girl's wardrobe.

Row 7: Cast off remaining 13 (13:13) stitches which are part of the neck shaping.

Rejoin wool to stitches left on needle and, remembering to always knit the 2 stitches at centre back edge on every row, complete to match the first half of the back.

(Note: shoulder shaping is reversed: **Row 1:** cast off 5 (5:6) stitches, PURL to last 2 stitches, knit 2 stitches).

FRONT: Work as back until work measures 7.5 (9:10)cm/3 (3^{1}/$_{2}$:4)in from start of armhole shaping, ignoring centre back neck split, and ending with a purl row.

SHAPE NECK: **Next row:** knit 23 (24:25) stitches, turn
Next row: purl. Continue on these stitches as follows:
Work 7 (7:7) rows, decreasing 1 stitch at neck edge on every row (3 stitches in from edge). *(16:17:18 stitches)*
Continue without shaping until armhole measures same as back, ending with a purl row.

SHAPE SHOULDER: **Next row:** cast off 5 (5:6) stitches, knit to end. **Next row:** purl. **Next row:** cast off 5 (6:6) stitches, knit to end. **Next row:** purl. **Next row:** cast off remaining 6 (6:6) stitches. With right side facing slip first 12 (12:12) stitches onto holder, rejoin yarn to remaining 23 (24:25) stitches and knit to end of row. **Next row:** purl. Work 7 (7:7) rows, decreasing 1 stitch at neck edge on every row (3 stitches in from edge). *(16 17:18 stitches)*
Continue without shaping until work measures same as back, ending with a knit row.
Shape shoulder to match first side (casting off on purl rows).

SLEEVES (TWO THE SAME): With 2.75mm (US 1) needles cast on 50 (54:58) stitches and work 2 (2:2)cm/^{3}/$_{4}$ (^{3}/$_{4}$:^{3}/$_{4}$)in, in knit 1, purl 1 rib.
Next row: rib 2 (4:6) ★increase in next stitch, rib 4, repeat from ★ to last 3 (5:7) stitches, increase in next stitch, rib 2 (4:6). *(60:64:68 stitches)*

left: A close-up of the neck opening. The split has been closed with a simple button and loop fastening, but you can stitch silk ribbon ties instead, if you prefer.

right (top): This little flower has been embroidered using the self yarn for the leaves and a toning ribbon for the two flowerheads.

right (centre): Knitted in lurex, this little sweater becomes a special party piece, particularly with a self-embroidered flower motif.

right (below): Knitted in a luxurious cashmere/angora blend, this classic pattern becomes an heirloom piece, to be handed down and treasured.

Change to 3.25mm (US 3) needles and continue in stocking (stockinette) stitch until work measures 5 (6.5:8)cm/2 (2^1/2:3)in from beginning.
SHAPE TOP OF SLEEVE: Cast off 1 stitch at beginning of next 2 rows to mark start of shaping. Now decrease 1 stitch at each end of next 11 (13:15) knit rows. *(36:36:36 stitches)* Purl 1 row. Decrease 1 stitch at each end of next 10 (10:10) rows. *(16:16:16 stitches)*
Cast off remaining stitches.

TO MAKE UP: Weave in all the ends. Lay work out flat, and steam each piece gently and press lightly to flatten out, avoiding the rib trims. Join the shoulder seams. Work the neckband as follows:
With 2.75mm (US 1) needles and right side of work facing pick up and knit 13 (13:13) stitches along left back neck, 18 (19:21) stitches along left side of neck, 12 (12:12) stitches from holder, 18 (19:21) stitches along right side of neck and 13 (13:13) stitches along right back neck. *(74:76:78 stitches)*. Work 2 rows in knit 1, purl 1 rib, cast off loosely in rib. (Tip: use 3.25mm (US 3) needles).

TO FINISH: Sew sleeves into armhole using a fine back-stitch. Using mattress stitch join side seams and sleeve seams. Sew on button and make button-loop for back neck fastening. Alternatively, sew ribbon/trim around neck and/or embroider.

Swiss-embroidered flower: If you wish to embroider the little flower onto your child's sweater, then trace the pattern from one of the images shown left, reduce or enlarge it to the appropriate size on a photocopier, and then stitch it using either the same yarn used for the pattern, or fine silk ribbon. Use a blunt-ended needle with a large eye. Place the flower below the left shoulder or above the rib hem.

denim pinafore

A reworking of the traditional pinafore, this dress is made in denim yarn, which shrinks after being washed for the first time, but not thereafter (the pattern has taken the shrinkage into account). It is sure to be a favourite as it is so versatile, and just that much more special than the ubiquitous denim jeans. Very simply made in stocking (stockinette) stitch with fully fashioned shaping details through the garment, to create a pretty 'A' line shape, it is trimmed with a picot edge at the hem, armholes and neckline.

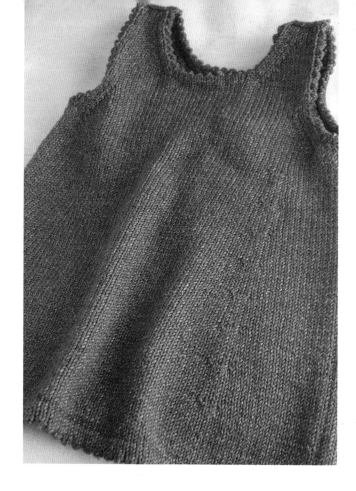

how to make **the denim pinafore**

MATERIALS: Medium-weight yarn (DK) e.g. Rowan denim knit yarn 100 per cent cotton • 6 (6:7) x 50g balls • Pair 3.25mm (US 3) needles • Pair 3.75mm (US 5) needles • Pair 4mm (US 6) needles • Spare needles • Stitch holders • Large sewing needle

SIZING: for sizing refer to chart on pages 14–15.

STITCH SIZE: This dress has a stitch size of 20 stitches and 28 rows to 10cm (4in) measured over stocking (stockinette) stitch using 4mm (US 6) needles (before washing).

METHOD: FRONT AND BACK THE SAME: With 3.75mm (US 5) needles cast on 93 (99:105) stitches loosely and

above: This little dress has a wonderfully simple shape, its slight 'A'-line form created by shaping within the garment. Finishing details include a picot-edged hem, armholes and neckline.

work 4 rows in stocking (stockinette) stitch.

Next row: knit 1 stitch ★ with the yarn forward, knit 2 stitches together, repeat from ★ to the end of the row.

Next row: purl.

Work 4 rows in stocking (stockinette) stitch.

Next row: make the picot hem by knitting together 1 stitch from the needle and 1 loop from the cast on edge all across the row.

Next row: purl.

Change to 4mm (US 6) needles and work 16 (16:16) rows in stocking (stockinette) stitch.

1st shaping row: knit 17 (19:21) stitches, knit 2 stitches together, knit 1 stitch, knit 2 stitches together through the back loop, knit 49 (51:53) stitches, knit 2 stitches together,

left: You can ring the changes
with T-shirts and blouses to
make this little dress either
casual or suitable for a party.
The unfussy neckline makes it
very easy to get on and off.

right: You can see here the delicate picot edging on the neck and armholes. Small finishing touches like these give simple garments the look of retro classics.

knit 1 stitch, knit 2 stitches together through the back loop, knit 17 (19:21) stitches. *(89:95:101 stitches)* Work 9 (9:9) rows in stocking (stockinette) stitch.

2nd shaping row: knit 16 (18:20) stitches, knit 2 stitches together, knit 1 stitch, knit 2 stitches together through the back loop, knit 47 (49:51) stitches, knit 2 stitches together, knit 1 stitch, knit 2 stitches together through the back loop, knit 16 (18:20) stitches. *(85:91:97 stitches)*

Continue decreasing 4 stitches on every following tenth row until 61 (67:73) stitches remain. (Remember to work 1 stitch less before decreasing and 2 stitches less in the middle to keep the centre stitch of the darts in line.)

Continue without shaping until work measures 37 (39:43)cm/14 ^{1}/2 (15^1/2:17)in, ending with a purl row.

SHAPE ARMHOLE: cast off 4 (4:4) stitches at the beginning of the next 2 rows, and then decrease 1 stitch (3 stitches in, see page 118) at each end of the next and every alternate row until 41 (45:49) stitches remain.

Continue without shaping until the armhole measures 8 (9.5:11)cm/3 ^{1}/4 (3^3/4:4 ^{1}/4)in, ending with a purl row.

SHAPE NECK: knit 15 (16:17) stitches, turn and leave the remaining stitches on a stitch holder

Next row: purl.

Now decrease 1 stitch (3 stitches in) at the neck edge on next and every alternate row until 8 (9:10) stitches remain. Continue without shaping until the armhole measures 16 (17.5:19)cm /6^1/4 (7:7^1/2)in.

Leave stitches on a spare needle.

Place the centre 11 (13:15) stitches on a holder. With right side facing, rejoin yarn to the remaining stitches, knit to the

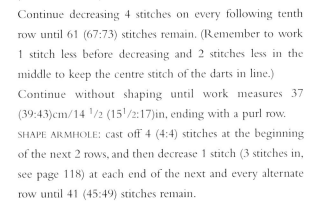

above: Fully fashioned shaping details, worked three stitches in from the edge, give an elegant touch to any garment.

end of the row. Complete to match the first side.

MAKE UP: Join one shoulder seam by grafting with two needles (see page 118), wrong sides together, to make seam detail on the right side.

NECK BORDER: With the right side facing, and using 3.25mm (US 3) needles, knit up 15 (16:17) stitches down the side of the neck, knit 11 (13:15) stitches from the holder, knit up 15 (16:17) stitches to the shoulder seam, 15 (16:17) stitches down the side of the neck, 11 (13:15) stitches from the holder and 15 (16:17) stitches up side of the neck. *(82:90:98 stitches)*

Next row: purl.

Next row: knit 1 stitch, ★ with the yarn forward, knit 2 stitches together, repeat from ★ to the last stitch, knit 1 stitch..

Next row: purl.

Next row: knit

Cast off purlwise.

Graft the second shoulder seam, in the same way as the first.

ARMHOLE BORDERS: With the right side facing and using 3.25mm (US 3) needles, pick up 68 (72:74) stitches around armhole. Work to match neck border.

TO FINISH: Weave in all the ends. Wash garment, with a little ball of yarn to sew up, at 60°C/140°F and tumble dry. Lay work out flat, and steam gently. Join the side seams using mattress stitch. Fold the picot edges of neck and armholes to the inside of dress and slip stitch into position.

girl's games sweater

Based on a traditional, school-sports' style, this tunic

sweater is immensely versatile and an all-time classic,

which makes it the perfect 'hand-me-down'. Make it

in cotton or fine wool. It is worked in stocking

(stockinette) stitch with a contrast-stitch collar and

hem. It has three-quarter-length sleeves and two

little pockets to give it simple but useful detailing.

The pattern comes in three sizes, but it is quite a

generous fit, so there will be ample room for growth

or for incorporating a little T-shirt or vest under it,

for chilly days.

how to make **the girl's games sweater**

above: Loose-fitting and roomy, this simple but elegant little sweater is ideal for energetic games.

MATERIALS: Fine yarn (4 ply yarn) e.g. Rowan 4 ply 100 per cent cotton (or Jaeger Matchmaker merino wool or Jaeger baby merino 4 ply • 6 (7:8) x 50g balls • Pair 3.25mm (US 3) needles; pair 2.75mm (US 1) needles • Coloured yarn for markers • Spare needles (for keeping stitches on when not in use) • Sewing needle

SWEATER SIZE: for sizing refer to chart on page 14–15.

STITCH SIZE: This sweater has a stitch size of 28 stitches and 36 rows to 10cm (4in) measured over stocking (stockinette) stitch, using 3.25mm (US 3) needles.

TIPS AND TECHNIQUES: If you wish, you could use an alternative stitch for the finishing details, instead of the garter stitch, shown here. Moss stitch (in which a knit 1, purl 1 row is alternated with a purl 1, knit 1 row) would be equally successfully.

METHOD: BACK: Using 2.75mm (US 1) needles, cast on 92 (100:108) stitches. Work 20 rows in garter stitch, every row knit. Change to 3.25mm (US 3) needles and stocking (stockinette) stitch. Contine until work measures 23 (24:25)cm/9 ($9^1/2$:10)in from the cast on edge, ending with a purl row.

SHAPE ARMHOLES: Cast off 7 (7:7) stitches at the beginning of the next 2 rows. *(78 86:94 stitches).*

Continue until work measures 35.5 (38:40.5)cm/14 (15:16)in, ending with a purl row.

Next row: knit 15 (18:22) stitches, cast off loosely 48 (50:50) stitches, knit to end. Leave stitches on a spare needle, for shoulder seams.

POCKET LININGS (TWO THE SAME): Using 3.25mm (US 3) needles cast on 22 (24:26) stitches and work 26 (30:34) rows in stocking (stockinette) stitch. Leave stitches on a spare needle.

FRONT: Using 2.75mm (US 1) needles, cast on 92 (100:108) stitches. Work 20 rows in garter stitch.

Change to 3.25mm (US 3) needles and stocking (stockinette) stitch. Work 20 (24:28) rows.

WORK POCKET TRIMS: **Row 1:** knit

Row 2: purl 9 (10:11) stitches, knit 22 (24:26) stitches, purl 30 (32:34) stitches, knit 22 (24:26) stitches, purl 9 (10:11) stitches.

Rows 3–8: as rows 1-2 three times.

PLACE POCKETS: **Row 1:** knit 9 (10:11) stitches, cast off 22 (24:26) stitches, knit 30 (32:34) stitches, cast off 22

above: Garter-stitch detailing on the collar, cuffs, hems and pockets add detail to this classic sweater. The pockets are knitted integrally with the body for a neater finish.

opposite: Three-quarter length sleeves complement this loose-fitting tunic-style sweater, while the grafted shoulder seams add a pretty finishing detail.

(24:26) stitches, knit 9 (10:11) stitches.

Row 2: purl 9 (10:11) stitches, purl 22 (24:26) stitches of pocket lining (on spare needle), purl 30 (32:34) stitches, purl 22 (24:26) stitches of pocket lining, purl 9 (10:11) stitches. Continue as for back.

GRAFT SHOULDER SEAM: Work 2 the same. Using 3.25mm (US 3) needles, put 15 (18:22) stitches from the back and the same from the front onto spare needles. Place these two needles side by side, with the wrong side of the work facing each other. Then working on the right side of the work, ★ knit together a stitch from each needle to give 1 stitch on the right-hand needle. Repeat from ★ (now 2 stitches on the right-hand needle), then pass the first of these 2 stitches over the second. Continue as set across shoulder stitches.

SLEEVES (TWO THE SAME): Using 2.75mm (US 1) needles cast on 53 (57:61) stitches. Work 20 rows in garter stitch. Change to 3.25mm (US 3) needles and stocking (stockinette) stitch.

Increase 1 stitch (2 stitches in – see page 118). at each end of the next row, and every following 5th row to 71 (77:85) stitches.

Continue without shaping until work measures 18(20:23)cm/7 (8:9)in: place coloured markers each end of last row.

Work 10 (10:10) rows straight to fit into armhole (like a kimono sleeve). Cast off.

COLLAR: With 2.75mm (US 1) needles cast on 100 (102: 102) stitches and work 10 (10:10) rows in knit 1, purl 1 rib, change to garter stitch and work a further 4.5 (5:5)cm/1³/₄(2:2)in. Cast off.

TO FINISH: Weave in all the ends. Lay work out flat, and steam each piece gently and press lightly to flatten out,

Set the sleeves into the armholes (see page 120), and backstitch into position.

Sew the sleeve and side-seams with mattress stitch (see page 119).

Sew pocket linings down on the inside neatly.

Fold collar in half and join the rib part.

Attach collar: mark centre front neck of sweater. Pin rib edge of collar to neck, having collar seam at centre front neck. Stitch into position using a flat seam all around neck edge. Fold over collar and allow to spread out.

fluffy bolero

This is the perfect alternative to the "little white cardigan". It is made in fluffy mohair for girlie appeal. Very soft and whisper light, it is a "must have" to wear over a party frock but looks good, too, as a contrast to jeans. It is very simple to knit, as it is made in one piece and has the minimum of sewing-up, so it is also very quick to make. Knitted in stocking (stockinette) stitch, it has a curved front edge with garter-stitch borders that contrast with the plain knitting. Although this one is knitted in go-with-anything white, it would look charming in pink or lilac.

how to make **the fluffy bolero**

MATERIALS: Medium-weight yarn, such as Jaeger Mohair art (50 per cent mohair: 50 per cent nylon) • 2 (2:3) x 50g balls of white • Pair 3.75mm (US 5) needles • Coloured yarn for markers • Sewing needle.

SIZING: Refer to charts on pages 14-15.

STITCH SIZE: This bolero has a stitch size of 25 stitches and 33 rows to 10cm (4in) measured over stocking (stockinette) stitch using 3.75mm (US 5) needles.

METHOD: RIGHT FRONT: Using 3.75 mm (US 5) needles cast on 21 (23: 25) stitches.

Shape front edge and work garter stitch border as follows:

Row 1: increase into first stitch, knit to end

Row 2: knit to last 2 stitches, increase into next stitch, knit 1 stitch.

Rows 3 to 8: repeat rows 1 and 2 three times. *(29:31:33 stitches)*

Row 9: knit 7 stitches, increase into the next stitch, and knit to the end.

Row 10: knit 1, purl to the last 7 stitches, knit 7 stitches.

Repeat rows 9 and 10 until there are 35 (38: 41) stitches Keeping the garter stitch border correct, continue as set until front measures 11.5 (12.5:14)cm/4^1/2 (5:5^1/2) in from the beginning, ending with a knit row.

SLEEVE SHAPING: **Row 1:** cast on 7 (8:9) stitches, knit 1 stitch, purl to the last 7 stitches, knit 7 stitches *(42:46:50 stitches)*. **Row 2:** knit. **Rows 3 and 4:** as rows 1 and 2 *(49:54:59 stitches)*. **Row 5:** cast on 7 (8:9) stitches, knit 7 stitches, purl to the last 7 stitches, knit 7 stitches. *(56: 62:68 stitches)*.

Row 6: knit.

NECK SHAPING: Knit 7 stitches, purl to the last 10 stitches, purl 2 stitches together, purl 1 stitch, knit 7 stitches.

Keeping the garter-stitch borders correct, work 3 rows straight. Repeat the last 4 rows until 49 (54:59) stitches remain. Work straight until the sleeve border measures 23 (25.5:28)cm/9 (10:11)in.

Place a coloured marker at each end of the last row to show the shoulder line. Work for a further 2.5cm (1in), ending with a purl row.

Break off the yarn and leave the stitches on a spare needle.

LEFT FRONT: Using 3.75mm (US 5) needles, cast on 21 (23:25) stitches. Shape the front edge and work in the garter-stitch border as follows:

Row 1: knit to the last 2 stitches, purl twice into the next stitch, knit 1 stitch. **Row 2:** increase into the first stitch, knit to the end. **Rows 3 to 8:** repeat rows 1 and 2 three times *(29:31:33 stitches)*. **Row 9:** knit to the last 9 stitches, increase into next stitch, knit to the end. **Row 10:** knit 7 stitches, purl to the last stitch, knit 1 stitch.

Repeat rows 9 and 10 until there are 35 (38:41) stitches.

Keeping the garter stitch border correct, continue as set until the front measures 11.5(12.5:14)cm/4^1/2 (5:5^1/2)in from the beginning ending with a purl row.

SLEEVE SHAPING: **Row 1:** cast on 7 (8:9) stitches, knit to the end. *(42:46:50 stitches)*. **Row 2:** knit 7 stitches, purl to the last stitch, knit1 stitch. **Rows 3 and 4:** as rows 1 and 2 *(49:54:59 stitches)*. **Row 5:** cast on 7 (8:9) stitches, knit to the end. *(56:62:68 stitches)*. **Row 6:** knit 7, purl to the last 7 stitches, knit 7 stitches.

NECK SHAPING: **Next row:** knit 7, knit to the last 10 stitches, knit 2 stitches together, knit to end.

Keeping the garter-stitch borders correct, work 3 rows

straight. Repeat the last 4 rows until 49 (54:59) stitches remain. Continue until the work measures 23 (25.5:28)cm/9 (10:11)in.

Place a coloured marker at each end of the last row to denote the shoulder line Work for a further 2.5cm (1in) ending with a purl row.

BACK: **Next row:** pattern across the left front to the last stitch, slip 1 stitch, turn and cast on 15 (17:19) stitches for the back neck. TURN, and with right side facing, pattern across the stitches of the right front from the spare needle *(113:125:137 stitches)*

NECK TRIM: **Row 1:** knit 7 stitches, purl 35 (40:45) stitches, knit 29 (31:33) stitches, purl 35 (40:45) stitches, knit 7 stitches.

Row 2: knit. **Rows 3 to 8:** work rows 1 and 2 twice more. **Next row:** knit 7 stitches, purl to the last 7 stitches, knit 7 stitches. Keeping garter-stitch border correct, continue until the back sleeve borders measure the same as the front sleeve borders (the coloured marker for shoulder line is at half-way point).

SLEEVE SHAPING: Cast off 7 (8:9) stitches at beginning of next 6 rows *(71:77:83 stitches)*. Continue in stocking (stockinette) stitch until back measures the same as fronts from underarm to beginning of garter-stitch border, ending with a purl row. Next row: knit to end. Repeat this row 7 times more and cast off knitwise.

TO MAKE UP: Join body and sleeve seams using mattress stitch (see page 119). Steam and press lightly.

dressing gown

Very simple in style, this cosy dressing gown is made in a beautiful natural blend of cotton and wool for both warmth and comfort in a simple generous wrap-over kimono style worked in stocking (stockinette) stitch with garter stitch trims. It has two little patch pockets in which to keep a tissue or the last piece of jigsaw, or that vital spare piece of Lego. You may wish to embroider the little cherub's name or initial on the pocket. The dressing gown is tied with either an easily made knitted cord or a bought silk one. This is the project any grandmother will be pleased to make, as it is wonderfully practical. Knitted here in flannel grey, it would look equally good in periwinkle blue or berry red.

left: Warm and cosy, in a generous kimono-style shape, this dressing gown is suitable for boys or girls (just alter the direction of the wrap). A silk or knitted cord can be used to keep the dressing gown snugly tied.

how to make **the dressing gown**

MATERIALS: Medium weight yarn e.g. Rowan wool cotton: 50 per cent merino/50 per cent cotton • 9 (10:10) x 50g balls • Pair 4mm (US 6) needles • Pair 3.75mm (US 5) needles • Sewing needle

DRESSING GOWN SIZE: for sizing refer to chart on pages 14–15.

STITCH SIZE: This dressing gown has a stitch size of 22 stitches and 30 rows to 10cm (4in) measured over stocking (stockinette) stitch using 4mm (US 6) needles.

METHOD: BACK: Using 3.75mm (US 5) needles cast on 103 (109:115) stitches. Work 12 rows in garter stitch, every row knit.
Change to 4mm (US 6) needles and stocking (stockinette) stitch.

Work 18 (20: 22) rows.
First shaping row: ★ knit 19 (20:21) stitches, knit 2 stitches together through the back loop, repeat from ★ once, knit 19 (21:23) stitches ★★ knit 2 stitches together, knit 19 (20:21) stitches, repeat from ★★ once.
Work 13 (15:17) rows of stocking (stockinette) stitch.
Second shaping row: ★ knit 18 (19: 20) stitches, knit 2 stitches together through the back of loop, repeat from ★ once, knit 19 (21: 23) stitches, ★★ knit 2 stitches together, knit 18 (19: 20) stitches, repeat from ★★ once.
Work 13 (15:17) rows of stocking (stockinette) stitch.
Third shaping row: ★ knit 17 (18: 19) stitches, knit 2 sitches together through the back of loop, repeat from ★ once, knit 19 (21:23) stiches, ★★ knit 2 stitches together, knit 17 (18:19) stitches, repeat from ★★ once. Work 13 (15:17) rows of stocking (stockinette) stitch.

left: The wrap-over edge of
the dressing gown is knitted in
garter stitch, to keep it firm.
Similar garter stitch detailing
edges the sleeves at the cuff
and the pocket tops.

Fourth shaping row: ★ knit 16 (17:18) stitches, knit 2 stitches together through the back loop, repeat from ★ once, knit 19 (21:23) stitches, ★★ knit 2 stitches together, knit 16 (17:18) stitches, repeat from ★★ once.

Work 13 (15:17) rows of stocking (stockinette) stitch.

Fifth shaping row: ★ knit 15 (16:17) stitches, knit 2 stitches together through the back loop, repeat from ★ once, knit 19 (21:23) stitches, ★★ knit 2 stitches together, knit 15 (16:17) stitches, repeat from ★★ once.

Work 13 (15:17) rows of stocking (stockinette) stitch.

Sixth shaping row: ★ knit 14 (15:16) stitches, knit 2 stitches together through the back loop, repeat from ★ once, knit 19 (21:23) stitches, ★★ knit 2 stitches together, knit 14 (15:16) stitches, repeat from ★★ once.

Work 13 (15:17) rows of stocking (stockinette) stitch.

Seventh shaping row: ★ knit 13 (14:15) stitches, knit 2 stitches together through the back loop, repeat from ★ once, knit 19 (21:23) stitches, ★★ knit 2 together, knit 13 (14:15) stitches, repeat from ★★ once. (75 81:87 stitches.)

Work 19 (21:23) rows of stocking (stockinette) stitch.

SHAPE ARMHOLES: **Rows 1 & 2:** cast off 6 (7:8) stitches at the beginning of each row. **Row 3:** knit 3 stitches, knit 2 stitches together, knit to the last 5 stitches, knit 2 stitches together through the back loop, knit 3 stitches. **Row 4:** purl. Repeat the 3rd and 4th rows twice more, and then work the third row again. (55:59:63 stitches).

above: When you knit this little dressing gown, check the sizing carefully to ensure a loose and comfortable fit. You can alter the length, if needed, very easily by simply adding more rows between the garment hem and armhole shaping.

Work 29 (33: 37) rows of stocking (stockinette) stitch

SHAPE SHOULDERS: cast off 5 (5:6) stitches at the beginning of the next 2 rows, 5 (6:6) stitches at the beginning of the following 2 rows, and 6 (6:6) stitches at the beginning of the next 2 rows.

Cast off remaining 23 (25:27) stitches.

LEFT FRONT: Using 3.75mm (US 5) needles cast on 75 (77:79) stitches and work 12 rows in garter stitch.

Change to 4mm (US 6) needles.

Row 1: knit.

Row 2: knit 8, purl to the end.

Repeat these 2 rows 8 (9:10) times more.

Keeping the continuity of the garter-stitch border, shape as follows:

First shaping row: ★ knit 19 (20:21) stitches, knit 2 stitches together through back loop, repeat from ★ once. Knit to the end of the row.

Work 13 (15:17) rows.

Second shaping row: ★ knit 18 (19:20) stitches, knit 2 stitches together through back loop, repeat from ★ once, knit to the end of the row.

Work 13 (15:17) rows.

Third shaping row: ★ knit 17 (18: 19) stitches, knit 2 stitches together, through back loop ,repeat from ★ once, knit to the end of the row.

Work 13 (15:17) rows.

Fourth shaping row: ★knit 16 (17:18) stitches, knit 2 stitches together through back loop, repeat from ★ once, knit to the end of the row..

Work 13 (15:17) rows.

Fifth shaping row: ★ knit 15 (16:17) stitches, knit 2 stitches together through back loop, repeat from ★ once, knit to the end of the row.

Work 13 (15:17) rows.

Sixth shaping row: ★ knit 14 (15:16) stitches, knit 2 stitches together through back loop, repeat from ★ once, knit to the end of the row.

Work 13 (15:17) rows.

Seventh shaping row: ★ knit 13 (14:15) stitches, knit 2 stitches together through back loop, repeat from ★ once, knit to the end of the row. *(61:63:65stitches).*

Work 1 (3:5) rows

SHAPE FRONT EDGE: **Row 1:** Knit to the last 10 stitches, knit 2 stitches together, knit 8 stitches.

Row 2: knit 8 stitches, purl to end of row.

Repeat these 2 rows 8 (8:8) times more. *(52 54:56 stitches)*

SHAPE ARMHOLE: **Row 1:** cast off 6 (7:8) stitches, knit to the last 10 stitches, knit 2 stitches together, knit 8 stitches.

Row 2: knit 8 stitches; purl to end of row.

Row 3: knit 3 stitches, knit 2 stitches together, knit to the last 10 stitches, knit 2 stitches together,, knit 8 stitches.

Repeat rows 2-3 three times more *(37:38:39 stitches).*

This completes the armhole shaping.

Continue to shape the front neck edge as follows:

Row 1: knit 8 stitches, purl to end of row.

Row 2: knit to the last 10 stitches knit 2 stitches together, knit 8 stitches.

Repeat these two rows 12 (12:12) times more. *(24:25:26 stitches).*

above: The full view of the dressing gown, knitted in stocking (stockinette) stitch in warm merino wool.

Work 3 (7:11) rows without shaping, ending at armhole edge.

SHAPE SHOULDER: Cast off 5 (5:6) stitches at the beginning of the next row, 5(6:6) stitches on the following alternate row and 6 (6:6) stitches on the next alternate row.

On the remaining 8 stitches continue in garter stitch for a further 20 (21: 22) rows for the neckband.

Cast off.

RIGHT FRONT: Using 3.75mm (US 5) needles cast on 75 (77:79) stitches and work 12 rows in garter stitch.

Change to 4mm (US 6) needles.

Row 1: knit.

Row 2: purl to the last 8 stitches, knit 8 stitches.

Repeat these 2 rows 8 (9:10) times more.

Keeping the continuity of the garter-stitch border, shape as follows:

First shaping row: knit 33 stiches, ★ knit 2 stitches together, knit 19 (20: 21) stitches, repeat from ★.

Work 13 (15:17) rows.

Second shaping row: knit 33 stitches, ★ knit 2 stitches together, knit 18 (19:20) stitches, repeat from ★.

Work 13 (15:17) rows.

Third shaping row: knit 33 stitches, ★ knit 2 stitches together, knit 17 (18:19) stitches, repeat from ★.

Work 13 (15:17) rows.

Fourth shaping row: knit 33 stitches, ★ knit 2 stitches together, knit 16 (17: 18), repeat from ★.

Work 13 (15:17) rows.

Fifth shaping row: knit 33 stitches, ★knit 2 stitches together, knit 15 (16:17) stitches, repeat from ★.

Work 13 (15:17) rows.

Sixth shaping row: knit 33 stitches, ★knit 2 stitches together, knit 14 (15:16) stitches, repeat from ★.

Work 13 (15:17) rows.

Seventh shaping row: knit 33 stitches, ★ knit 2 stitches together, knit 13 (14: 15) stitches, repeat from ★. *(61:63: 65 stitches)*.

Work 1 (3:5) rows.

SHAPE FRONT EDGE: **Row 1:** knit 8 stitches, knit 2 stitches together through back loop, knit to the end of the row.

Row 2: purl to the last 8 stitches, knit 8 stitches.

Repeat these 2 rows 8 (8:8) times more then work the first row again. *(51 (53: 55 stitches)*.

SHAPE ARMHOLE: **Row 1:** cast off 6 (7:8) stitches, purl to the last 8 stitches, knit 8 stitches.

Row 2: knit 8 stitches; knit 2 stitches together through the back loop, knit to the last 5 stitches, knit 2 stitches together through the back loop,

knit 3 stitches.

Row 3: purl to the last 8 stitches, knit 8 stitches.

Repeat the second and third rows twice more, then work the second row again. *(37 38:39 stitches.)*

This completes the armhole shaping.

Continue to shape the front neck edge as follows:

Row 1: purl to the last 8 stitches, knit 8 stitches.

Row 2: knit 8 stitches, knit 2 stitches together through back loop, knit to the end.

Repeat these two rows 12 (12:12) times more. *(24 :25:26 stitches).*

Work 4 (8:12) rows without shaping, ending at armhole edge.

SHAPE SHOULDER: Cast off 5 (5:6) stitches at the beginning of the next row, 5 (6:6) stitches on the following alternate row and 6 (6:6) stitches on the next alternate row.

On the remaining 8 stitches continue in garter stitch for a further 20 (21: 22) rows for the neckband. Cast off.

far left: A close up of the garter stitch border, used for the front edges and the hem of the gown. Knitted on a size smaller needle, they create a neat, firm texture.

left: The patch pockets (one on each front) are similarly finished with a few rows of garter stitch at the top of each pocket.

left: Small belt loops stitched to the side seams of the dressing gown hold the cord securely in place. Choose from a silk cord, as here, or a knitted rouleau (see page 119).

SLEEVES (TWO THE SAME): Using 3.75mm (US 5) needles, cast on 41 (43: 45) stitches. Work 12 rows in garter stitch.

Change to 4mm (US 6) needles and stocking (stockinette) stitch, work 4 rows. Increase 1 stitch at each end of next and every following sixth row to 61 (65: 67) stitches.

Work straight until sleeve measures 24 (27:29)cm/9^1/2 (10^1/2:11^1/2)in ending with a purl row. Place markers at each end of last row. Work 8 (8:8) more rows.

SHAPE TOP: **Row 1:** knit 3 stitches, knit 2 stitches together, and knit to the last 5 stitches, knit 2 sitches together through back loops, knit 3stitches. **Row 2:** purl.

Repeat these 2 rows until 53 (57:59) stitches remain. Cast off.

POCKETS: Using 4 mm (US 6) needles cast on 15 (16:17) stitches and work 2 (2:2) rows in stocking (stockinette) stitch. Increase 1 stitch (2 stitches in) at each end of the next three alternate rows. *(21: 22: 23 stitches).*

Continue in stocking (stockinette) stitch until pocket measures 9 (10:11)cm/3^1/2(4:4)in, ending with a knit row. Change to 3.75 mm (US 5) needles and work 6 rows in garter stitch. Cast off.

BELT LOOPS (MAKE TWO): Using 3.75mm (US 5) needles cast on 11 stitches and work 3 rows in garter stitch. Cast off.

TO MAKE UP: Weave in all the ends. Lay work out flat, and steam each piece gently and press lightly to flatten out, avoiding the garter stitch trims. Join shoulder seams. Set the sleeves into the armholes, in between cast offs for armholes (kimono style). Sew with mattress stitch (see page 119). Sew the sleeve and side seams in the same way. Sew the front strapping into position around back neck, and join at the centre back with a flat seam. Sew the belt loops to side seams. Sew on the pockets to left and right fronts. Make a knitted rouleau for the belt (see page 119) or buy a silk cord.

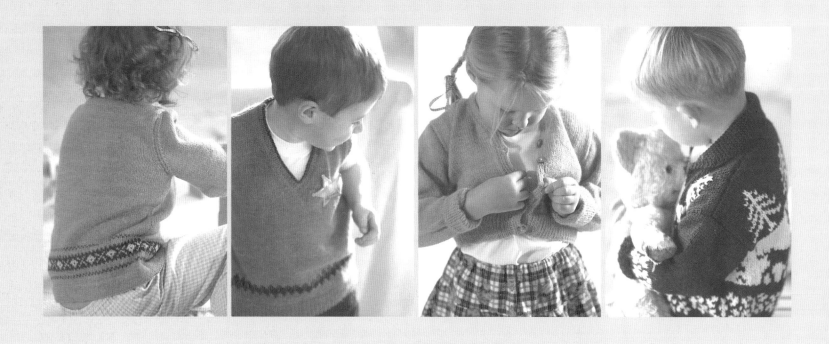

patterned classics

scottie dog cardigan

Typically retro, in soft oatmeal marl merino yarn, this little cardigan spells instant nostalgia. The cardigan has a classic V-neck and turned back cuff details. Make it with your favourite motif: a little Scottie dog or perhaps a small rose. The motif is worked on a patch pocket and stitched on afterwards, although you can easily knit this with the main body if you prefer. The back and fronts of this cardigan are worked together to avoid sewing up which also gives a lovely seam-free detail – perfect if you wish to create a little row of Scotties all around the cardigan itself (see the Fairisle border cardigan on pages 62-7). If the elbows wear, darn them or make patches to keep this cherished piece in your children's lives.

right: If you wish, you can finish the neck and button-band with checked or plain ribbon, to reinforce the seams and strengthen the buttonband.

opposite: The V-neck is easy to wear (it will slip over the head without unbuttoning) and the single pocket with its little motif adds a nice retro touch to this classic pattern.

how to make **the scottie dog cardigan**

MATERIALS: Fine yarn (4 ply yarn) such as Jaeger matchmaker merino 100 per cent merino wool • Colour A: oatmeal 4 (4:5) x 50g balls • Colour B: anthracite 1 x 50g balls • Colour C: peony – the smallest scrap • Colour D: cream – the smallest scrap • Pair 3mm (US 2) needles • Pair 3.25mm (US 3) needles • 5 buttons • Coloured yarn for markers • Sewing needle

SIZING: for sizing for the cardigan refer to the chart on pages 14–15.

STITCH SIZE: 28 stitches and 36 rows to 10cm (4in) measured over stocking (stockinette) stitch, using 3.25mm (US 3) needles.

TIPS: You could change the motif to a little flower, if you want a more femine look for the cardigan (see page 61 for an alternative).

METHOD: FRONTS AND BACK (WORKED TOGETHER): Using 3mm (US 2) needles and colour A, cast on 162 (176:190) stitches. Work in knit 1, purl 1 rib for 4 (4.5:5)cm/1½ (1¾:2)in. Change to 3.25mm (US 3) needles. Knit 1 row; increase 1 stitch at centre. *(163:177:191 stitches)*.

Work in stocking (stockinette) stitch, beginning with a purl row, until the work measures 18 (20:21.5)cm/7 (7¾:8½)in from the cast on edge, ending with a purl row.

Now divide the stitches for the back and fronts.

ARMHOLE SHAPING: **Next row:** knit 36 (39:42) stitches, cast off 7 (8:9) stitches, knit 77 (83:89) stitches (counting stitch on the right needle), cast off 7 (8:9)stitches, and knit to the end of the row.

Work on the last set of 36 (39: 42) stitches for the left front. ** Decrease 1 stitch at both ends of the next row. Now decrease 1 stitch at the armhole (inner edge) on the next 2 rows.

Decrease 1 stitch at both ends of the next row. *(30:33:36 stitches)* This completes the armhole shaping.

Continue to decrease 1 stitch at the front edge on every third row 11 (11:12) times more. *(19:22:24 stitches)*

Continue without shaping until work measures 30.5 (32:34)cm/ 12 (12½:13½)in from the cast on edge, ending at the armhole edge.

SHAPE SHOULDER: cast off 10 (11:12) stitches at the beginning of the next row. Work 1 row. Cast off. ★★

With the wrong side of the work facing, rejoin the yarn to the centre 77 (83:89) stitches for the back. Purl 1 row.

Decrease 1 stitch at both ends of the next and every following alternate row, 5 times. *(67:73:79 stitches).*

Continue in stocking (stockinette) stitch until the work measures 30.5 (32:34)cm/12 (12½:13½)in, ending with a purl row. Shape shoulders by casting off 10 (11:12) stitches at the beginning of the next 2 rows. Cast off 9 (11:12) stitches at the beginning of the next two rows. Cast off.

With the wrong side of work facing, rejoin yarn to the armhole (inner edge) of the remaining 36 (39: 42) stitches.

Repeat from ★★ to ★★ as for the left side.

SLEEVES (TWO THE SAME): Using 3mm (US 2) needles, cast on 48 (50:52) stitches. Work in knit 1 purl, 1 rib for 4: (4.5: 5)cm/1½ (1¾ :2)in.

Change to 3.25mm (US 3) needles. Knit 1 row; increase 1

above: A close up of the knit 1, purl 1 rib of the cuff and hem of the cardigan. It creates a close-fitting but comfortably stretchy edge to the knitting.

stitch in the centre of the row. Work in stocking (stockinette) stitch, beginning with a purl row and increase 1 stitch at both ends of next and every following sixth row 12 (13:14) times. *(73:77:81 stitches).*

Continue without shaping until the sleeve measures 28 (31:35.5) cm/11 (12¼:14)in, ending with a purl row. Shape top by decreasing 1 stitch at both ends of the next 22 (24:26) rows. *(29:29:29 stitches).* Cast off.

BUTTONBANDS: sew the shoulder seams using mattress stitch (see page 120).

Using 3mm (US 3) needles and colour A, cast on 6 stitches. Work 2 rows in knit 1, purl 1 rib.

BUTTONHOLE ROW (outer edge): Knit 1 stitch, purl 1 stitch, knit 2 stitches together, wool forward (to make a stitch), knit 1 stitch, purl 1 stitch.

Work 15 (17:19) rows in knit 1, purl 1 rib.

Repeat the last 16 (18:20) rows 4 more times (this makes 5 buttonholes). Continue in rib until the band, when slightly stretched, is long enough to go up the left front, across the back of the neck and down the right front. Cast off.

POCKET: Using 3.25mm (US 3) needles and colour A, cast on 23 stitches and work in stocking (stockinette) stitch for 20 rows; at the same time, if knitting the motif in, refer to the chart given for the pocket on page 126, working the knit rows from right to left and the purl rows from left to right.

Count every square as a stitch and every square as a row. Change to 3 mm (US 2) needles and work 5 rows in knit 1, purl 1 rib.

Cast off in rib.

If you chose to embroider the motif in, follow the chart using the colours for the motif selected.

MAKE UP: Weave in all the ends. Lay work out flat, steam each piece gently and press lightly to flatten out, avoiding the rib trims.

Set the sleeves into the armholes, and sew with mattress stitch (see page 119). Sew the sleeve seams in the same way. Sew the front band into position, with the buttonholes to the right front for a girl and to the left front for a boy. Sew on the pocket.

FINISH: Sew on buttons in correct positions to correspond with facing buttonholes.

opposite: Alternatives to the motif are (right): a reversal of the main pattern, with the cardigan knitted in anthracite, and the Scottie in oatmeal and (below right) a little rose motif in violet with a pink centre, knitted on an oatmeal ground.

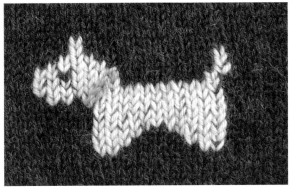

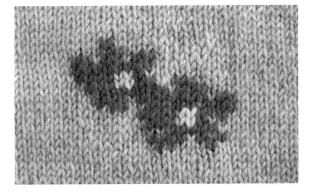

fairisle border cardigan

This classic little button-up cardigan has a simple round neck and an old-fashioned Fairisle pattern border. It is knitted in fine merino wool in a warm oatmeal mix: the Fairisle design is worked in four toning colours. The button band is trimmed with the traditional grosgrain ribbon, but you could chose gingham or velvet to create an entirely different effect. This cardigan has been designed with a hem, but could easily be worked in knit 1, purl 1 rib instead, to complement the short-sleeve sweater and create a twin- set. As a classic, you can make it time and time again, in a variety of ways, changing colours to suit your child's wardrobe.

left: The simple Fairisle border near the hem of the sweater, and the neat hem itself, with its garter stitch edge, give this little classic cardigan an elegant finishing touch.

how to make **the fairisle border cardigan**

MATERIALS: Fine yarn (4 ply yarn) e.g. Jaeger matchmaker merino 100 per cent merino wool • Colour A: oatmeal 4 (4:5) x 50g balls • Col B: strawberry 1 x 50g ball • Colour C: heather 1 x 50 g ball • Col D: cyclamen 1 x 50 g ball • Colour E: cream 1 x 50 g ball • Pair 3mm (US 2) needles • Pair 2.75mm (US 1) needles • Pair 3.25mm (US 3) needles • 7 buttons • Stitch holder • 2 safety pins • Coloured yarn for markers • Sewing needle • 1m (36in) grosgrain ribbon 1.5cm (³⁄₄in) wide.

SIZING: for sizing refer to chart on pages 14–15.

STITCH SIZE: 28 stitches and 36 rows to 10cm (4in) measured over stocking (stockinette) stitch using 3.25mm (US 3) needles.

METHOD:

BACK: Using 3mm (US 2) needles and colour A, cast on 80 (86: 92) stitches loosely. Work in stocking (stockinette) stitch for 2.5cm (1in), ending with a purl row. Using 2.75mm (US 1) needles, purl the next row of stitches instead of knitting them to create a neat turning row. Change to 3mm (US 2) needles and work another 2.5cm (1in), in stocking (stockinette) stitch ending with a purl row. Make the hem by knitting together one stitch from the needle and one loop from the cast-on edge all across the row.

Next row: purl.

Change to 3.25mm (US 3) needles and work 2 rows in stocking (stockinette) stitch. Work 19 rows Fairisle border (see chart on page 126), starting and finishing as indicated and working the 10-stitch repeat 8 (8:9) times.

Row 20: using colour A, purl.

Continue in stocking (stockinette) stitch until the work measures 21.5 (23:24) cm/8¹⁄₂ (9:9¹⁄₂)in from the turning row.

SHAPE ARMHOLES: Cast off 6 (7:8) stitches at the beginning of the next 2 rows. Decrease 1 stitch at each end of the next 6 rows. *(56:60:64 stitches.)* (Work the decreases 3 stitches in from the edge to give a fully fashioned detail, as discussed on page 118.)

left: The buttonband, and the inside neck, have been edged in gingham ribbon. The ribbon not only creates a neat finishing detail, it strengthens the buttonband and helps to hold its shape.

Continue without shaping until the armhole measures 13 (14:15)cm/5 (5½:6)in, ending with a purl row.

SHAPE SHOULDERS: Cast off 5 (5:6) stitches at the beginning of the next 2 rows. Cast off 5 (6:6) stitches at the beginning of the next 2 rows. Cast off 6 (6:6) stitches at the beginning of the next two rows. Leave the remaining 24 (26:28) stitches on a stitch holder.

LEFT FRONT: Using colour A and 3mm (US 2) needles, loosely cast on 37 (40: 43) stitches. Work 2.5 (2.5:2.5)cm/1 (1:1)in in stocking (stockinette) stitch, ending with a purl row.

Change to 2.75mm (US 1) needles and purl across the row, casting on 6 (6:6) stitches for the buttonband at the end of this row. (This gives a neat edge and avoids extra sewing up). Change to 3mm (US 2) needles. Work 2.5 (2.5:2.5)cm/1 (1:1)in in stocking (stockinette) stitch, with the 6 stitches for the button band in knit 1, purl 1 rib, ending with purl row. Make the hem as for the back, rib last 6 stitches. **Next row:** rib 6 stitches, purl to end.

Change to 3.25 mm (US 3) needles and continue in stocking (stockinette) stitch and rib for the buttonband. Work 2 rows.

Follow the Fairisle pattern for the border (see page 126), working the repeat 3 (4:4) times and continue with the buttonband, working colours as indicated. Continue until

top left: A close up of the Fairisle pattern, worked in another colourway, shows the stranding technique used when working in colours (see page 118).

above: The decreasing for the cardigan fronts have been worked three stitches in from the outside edge, to create a fully fashioned detail (see page 118).

top right: Classic pearl buttons complement this traditional-style cardigan beautifully, but you can choose buttons with a motif if you prefer.

knitting measures 21.5 (23:24) cm/9 (10:11)in from turning row, ending with a purl row.

SHAPE ARMHOLE: Cast off 6 (7:8) stitches at the beginning of the next row. **Next row:** purl. Now decrease 1 stitch (3 stitches in from the edge as on back) at the armhole edge until 32 (33:34) stitches remain.

Continue without further shaping until armhole measures 7 (9:10)cm/3 (3½:4)in, ending at the centre front edge.

SHAPE NECK: ★★Rib 6 stitches and leave these on a safety pin or spare length of thread.

Decrease 1 stitch at the neck edge (3 stitches in) on every row until 16 (17:18) stitches remain.

Continue straight until the armhole measures the same as the back, finishing at the armhole edge.

SHAPE SHOULDER: Cast off 5 (5:6) stitches at the beginning of the next row. **Next row:** purl. **Next row:** cast off 5 (6:6) stitches at the beginning of the next row. **Next row:** purl. **Next row:** cast off.★★

RIGHT FRONT: Mark positions for 6 buttons on the left front. The first 1cm (½in) from the turning row, the 6th 4cm (1¾in) from the safety pin; the 2nd, 3rd, 4th and 5th at evenly spaced intervals (approximately 5cm/2½in) along the buttonband.

Using colour A and 3mm (US 2) needles, cast on 37 (40:43) stiches loosely. Work 2.5 (2.5:2.5)cm/1 (1:1)in in stocking

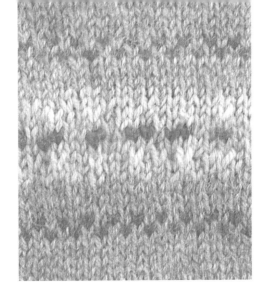

(stockinette) stitch, ending on a purl row.

Change to 2.75mm (US 1) needles. Cast on 6 stitches (for the buttonhole band), ★ knit 1 stitch, purl 1 stitch ★ three times, purl to end.

Change to 3mm (US 2) needles and work 3 rows of stocking (stockinette) stitch (starting with a purl row) with a 6-stitch knit 1, purl 1 rib buttonhole band.

Next row: make buttonhole: knit 1 stitch, purl 1 stitch, knit 2 stitches together, knit 1 stitch, purl 1 stitch, knit to end. Continue until work measures 2.5 (2.5:2.5)cm/1 (1:1)in from turning row. **Next row:** rib 6 stitches, make hem as for back. **Next row:** purl to last 6 stitches, rib 6 stitches.

Change to 3.25mm (US 3) needles and continue in stocking (stockinette) stitch and rib for the buttonhole band. Work 2 rows. Work the Fairisle pattern for the border (see chart) working the repeat 3 (4:4) times and making a buttonhole as before to match marked position on left front. Continue until knitting measures 21.5 (23:24)cm/8½ (9:9½)in, making further buttonholes as marked, and ending with a knit row.

SHAPE ARMHOLE: Cast off 6 (7:8) stitches at the beginning of the next two rows. Now decrease 1 stitch (3 stitches in) at armhole edge until 32 (33:34) stitches remain. Continue without further shaping until armhole measures 13 (14:15)cm/5 (5½:6)in, making futher buttonholes as marked, and ending with a knit row.

SHAPE NECK AND SHOULDER: As for left front from ★★ to ★★.

SLEEVES (TWO THE SAME): Using 2.75mm (US 2) needles cast on 48 (50:52) stitches and work in knit 1, purl 1 rib for 20 (22:24) rows.

Change to 3.25mm (US 3) needles and stocking (stockinette) stitch. Increase 1 stitch (3 stitches in)

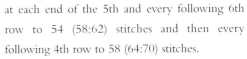
above: Blues, greens and oatmeals on a marled grey base would turn this little cardigan into one for a little boy.

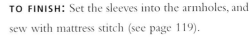
below: Mauves, pale greens and pinks on a soft blue base make a more feminine version of the cardigan.

at each end of the 5th and every following 6th row to 54 (58:62) stitches and then every following 4th row to 58 (64:70) stitches.

Continue without further shaping until work measures 23 (27:31)cm/9 (10½:12)in ending with a purl row.

SHAPE THE TOP: Cast off 1 stitch at the beginning of the next 2 rows, then decrease 1 stitch (3 stitches in) at each end of the next alternate 12 (13:14) rows. *(32:36:40 stitches.)* **Next row:** purl. Now decrease 1 stitch (3 stitches in) at each end of the next 8 (10:12) rows. *(16:16:16 stitches).* Cast off.

MAKE UP: Weave in all the ends. Lay work out flat, and steam press each piece gently, avoiding the rib trims. Join shoulder seams.

NECKBAND: Using 2.75mm (US 1) needles and with right side of the work facing, rib across 6 stitches, of buttonhole band, pick up and knit 22 (22:22) stitches along the right side of the neck, 24 (26:28) stitches from the stitch holder at the back, 22 (22:22) stitches down the left neck, then rib 6 stitches across the buttonband. *(80:82:84 stitches.)* Rib 3 rows. **Row 4:** make last buttonhole. **Row 5:** rib across stitches. Cast off in rib.

TO FINISH: Set the sleeves into the armholes, and sew with mattress stitch (see page 119).

Sew the sleeve seams and side seams in the same way. Sew the grosgrain ribbon into position on the inside of front bands and sew all around buttonhole. Sew buttons on other side to correspond with buttonholes. Turn back cuffs.

boy's diamond pullover

Reminiscent of school days, this little pullover is both practical and stylish. Classically retro, a real 'boy's own' design in soft grey fine merino yarn, it brings back instant memories. Knitted in stocking (stockinette) stitch with a little diamond pattern border in three vintage colours, with accented rib trims tipped in complementary colours. Very simple to make, it looks equally effective in brighter colours, or in shades of toning colours.

how to make **the boy's diamond pullover**

MATERIALS: Fine yarn (4 ply yarn) e.g. Jaeger Matchmaker merino 100 per cent merino wool or 4 ply soft or baby merino • Colour A: flannel grey 3 (3:4) x 50g balls • Colour B: beetroot 1 (1:1) x 50g ball • Colour C: spruce 1 (1:1) x 50g ball • Colour D: blue 1 (1:1) x 50g ball • Pair 2.75mm (US 1) needles • Pair 3.25mm (US 3) needles • Spare needles • Sewing needle

SIZE: For sizing refer to charts on pages 14–15.

STITCH SIZE: This pullover has a stitch size of 28 stitches and 36 rows to 10cm (4in) measured over stocking (stockinette) stitch using 3.25mm (US 3) needles.

TECHNIQUES: The simple Fairisle-style pattern above the hem is worked from the chart on page 126. When working from a chart, work the knit rows from right to left and the purl rows from left to right.

METHOD: BACK: Using 2.75mm (US 1) needles and colour B, cast on 84 (88:92) stitches. Work 1 row in knit 1, purl 1 rib. Change to colour A, and continue in rib until work measures 4 (4:4.5)cm/1^1/$_2$ (1^1/$_2$:1^3/$_4$)in. Change to 3.25mm (US 3) needles and stocking (stockinette) stitch and work 4 (4:6) rows.

Now knit the diamond border pattern from the chart on page 123 (4 stitch repeats and 11 rows). Working the knit rows from right to left and the purl rows from left to right,

above and right. This classic design, knitted in soft merino wool, is ideal for casual wear. It is simple to knit, with an easy-to-work Fairisle pattern just above the ribbed hem, and an attractively tipped rib in a contrasting colour.

join in colours as required. Continue in colour A until work measures 21.5 (23:24)cm/8^1/$_2$ (9:9^1/$_2$)in from the beginning, and ending with a purl row.

SHAPE ARMHOLE: Cast off 5 (5:5) stitches at the beginning of the next 2 rows.

Decrease 1 stitch (3 stitches in, see page 118) at each end of the next and every row until 52 (56:60) stitches remain.

Continue without shaping until the armhole measures 11 (13:14)cm/4 ^{1}/$_2$ (5:5^1/$_2$)in.

SHAPE SHOULDER: Cast off 5 (5:5) stitches at the beginning of the next 4 (4:4) rows. Cast off 6 (7:8) stitches at the beginning of the next 2 (2:2) rows. Leave the remaining 20 (22:24) stitches on a spare needle.

FRONT: Work as for the back until the armhole shaping. Shape the armhole and divide for the neck.

Row 1: cast off 5 (5:5) stitches, knit 36 (38:40) stitches (not including stitch already on right needle). TURN.

Leave the remaining 42 (44:46) stitches on a spare needle.

Next row: purl 3 stitches, purl 2 stitches together through the back of the loop, purl to the end of the row.

Continue in stocking (stockinette) stitch, decreasing 1 stitch (3 stitches in) at the armhole edge on every row, AT THE SAME TIME decreasing 1 stitch through the back of the loop at the neck edge (3 stitches in) on every following 3rd row until 22 (24:26) stitches remain.

Continue, decreasing 1 stitch at the neck edge on every

following 3rd row until 16 (17:18) stitches remain.

Continue without further shaping until the armhole matches the back, ending with a purl row.

SHAPE SHOULDER: Cast off 5 (5:5) stitches at the beginning of the next and following alternate row. Work 1 row. Cast off 6 (7:8) stitches.

With the right side facing, rejoin yarn to the remaining 42 (44:46) stitches.

Row 1: knit.

Row 2: cast off 5 (5:5) stitches, purl to the last 5 stitches, purl 2 stitches together, purl 3 stitches.

Continue, decreasing 1 stitch at the armhole edge (3 stitches in) on every row, AT THE SAME TIME decreasing at the neck edge on every 3rd row, until (22:24:26 stitches) remain.

Continue, decreasing 1 stitch at the neck edge on every following 3rd row until 16 (17:18) stitches remain.

Continue without shaping until the armhole measures the back, ending with a knit row.

Cast off 5 (5:5) stitches, in purl, at the beginning of the next 2 alternate rows. Work 1 row. Cast off 6 (7:8) stitches.

TO MAKE UP: Weave in all ends, lay work out flat and steam and press lightly, avoiding the rib bands. Join the right shoulder seam with backstitch.

NECKBAND: Using 2.75mm (US 1) needles and colour A, and with the right side of the work facing you, pick up and knit 44 (48:52) stitches along the left side of the neck, 1 stitch from the centre of the 'V', 44 (48:52) stitches along the right side of the neck and knit across 20 (22:24) stitches from the spare needle at the back neck. *(109:119:129 stitches).*

left: Small finishing touches, like the contrasting colour worked around the V-neck and hem, give this classic vest a special touch,

top right: The V-neck is worked with the decreases made three stitches in from the edge, giving a fully fashioned detail.

bottom right: The armhole edge, worked in one of the other colours in the Fairisle border, has the same fully fashioned decrease detail as the V-neck.

Row 1: purl 1 stitch, ★ knit 1 stitch, purl 1 stitch, repeat from ★ to end.

Row 2: ★ knit 1 stitch, purl 1 stitch ★ 21 (23:25) times, knit 2 stitches together through the back of the loop, knit 1 stitch, knit 2 stitches together, rib to the end.

Row 3: ★ purl 1 stitch, knit 1 stitch ★ 31 (34:37) times, purl 3 stitches, rib to the end.

Row 4: knit 1 stitch, ★ purl 1 stitch, knit 1 stitch ★ 20 (22:24) times, purl 2 stitches together, knit 1 stitch, purl 2 stitches together through the back of the loop, rib to the end.

Change to colour D and repeat row 1.

Cast off in colour D loosely, or use size 3.25mm (US 3) needles).

Join the left shoulder seam and neckband.

ARMHOLE BAND: Using 2.75mm (US 1) needles and colour A, pick up and knit 86 (92:98) stitches evenly all around the armhole edge

Row 1: ★ knit 1 stitch, purl 1 stitch,, repeat from ★ to the end of the row.

Row 2, 3, and 4: rib as set in colour A.

Row 5: rib as set in colour C.

Cast off in colour C loosely or use a size larger needle.

TO FINISH: Join the side seams with mattress stitch (see page 119). Steam and press the garment gently.

reindeer zipper cardigan

Inspired by the wonderful knitting patterns of the 1950s, this zipper cardigan is always popular. Worked in two colours, in chunky wool, it takes no time at all to make. With its Scandinavian-style reindeer and tree motifs, this style looks good in black and ecru. It has two integral pockets, a zipper fastener and a retro-style garter stitch collar. This cardigan will be handed down to little brothers and cousins until it wears out, so why not knit two little elbow patches to make it last that little bit longer?

how to make **the reindeer zipper cardigan**

left: The strong graphic pattern runs cross both front and back of the cardigan, in neat horizontal bands, alternative black or navy on ecru and ecru on black or navy. A neat rolled collar and a zipper provide the finishing details.

right: The back view of the cardigan in the navy and ecru version, with its two facing reindeer and neat rows of Christmas trees.

MATERIALS: Chunky yarn e.g. Jaeger Matchmaker merino 100 per cent merino wool • Colour A: black or navy 5 (6:7) x 50g balls • Colour B: ecru 2 (3:4) x 50g balls • Pair 4 mm (US 6) needles • Pair 4.5mm (US 7) needles • 30 cm (12in) open-ended zipper • Coloured yarn for markers • Spare needles • Sewing needle.

SIZING: for sizing refer to chart on pages 14–15.

STITCH SIZE: This cardigan has a stitch size of 19 stitches and 25 rows to 10cm (4in) measured over pattern using 4.5 mm (US 7) needles.

TIPS: Work the sleeves at the same time. Use a separate ball of yarn for each sleeve and drop it and start the next sleeve by picking up the other ball. To work from a chart, see pages 118 and 126-7. When working the reindeer motif (see Section 2 of pattern) take both yarns to each end of every row to maintain an even tension in this part of the garment. To make it easier to put in the zipper, two stitches have been added to each front (to be worked in garter stitch, every knit row).

METHOD: BACK: With 4mm (US 6) needles and colour A, cast on 56 (60:66) stitches. Work in knit 1, purl 1 rib for 4.5 (4.5:4.5)cm/2 (2:2)in.

Increase row: rib 3 (5:8) stitches, ★ increase into the next stitch, rib 7 stitches, repeat from ★ to the last 5 (7:10) stitches, increase into the next stitch, rib 4 (6:9) stitches. *(63:67:73 stitches).*

Change to 4.5mm (US 6) needles, and work in stocking (stockinette) stitch. Using stranding technique (see page 118) work from the chart (see page 127) to completion of

section 3, noting colour changes and ignoring pocket trims. Using colour A, work a further 8 (12:16) rows in stocking (stockinette) stitch.

SHAPE SHOULDER: Cast off 10 (11:12) stitches at the beginning of the next 4 rows. Cast off the remaining 23 (23:25) stitches.

POCKET LININGS (MAKE TWO): Using 4.5mm (US 7) needles and colour A, cast on 17 (17:17) stitches and work in stocking (stockinette) stitch for 14 (16:18) rows, leave the stitches on spare needle.

RIGHT FRONT: Using 4mm (US 6) needles and colour A cast on 28 (30:33) stitches and work in knit 1, purl 1 rib, for 4.5 (4.5:4.5)cm/2 (2:2)in.

Increase row: rib 1 (2:4) stitches ★ increase into the next stitch, rib 7 stitches, repeat from ★ to the last 3 (4:5) stitches, increase into the next stitch, rib 2 (3:4) stitches. *(32:34:37 stitches).* Change to 4.5mm (US 7) needles and stocking (stockinette) stitch. Work 10 (12:14) rows from the chart, remembering to work the 2 centre front stitches of every row in garter stitch and in main colour. Using colour A, over the next 4 rows, work 17 (17:17) stitches marked on chart in garter stitch for the pocket trim.

Next row: knit 8 (8:8) stitches, cast off 17 (17:17) stitches, knit to end. Change to colour B as the main colour and start section 2, placing the pocket lining in place of the stitches cast off on the previous row. Continue to work from the chart to the completion of Section 3 (ignoring part tree in Section 3). Using colour A, work a further 2 (6:10) rows in stocking (stockinette) stitch, ending with a purl row.

SHAPE NECK: ★ Cast off 8 (8:8) stitches at the beginning of the next row, then decrease 1 stitch at the neck edge on each row until 20 (22:24) stitches remain. Work 2 (2:1) more rows, ending with a knit row.

SHAPE SHOULDER: Cast of 10 (11:12) stitches at the beginning of the next and following alternate row★.

LEFT FRONT: Work as for right front, noting that the pocket top cast off is knit 7 (9:12) stitches, cast off 17 (17:17) stitches, knit to end. Continue to completion of Section 3.

Using colour A, work 1 (5:9) more rows in stocking (stockinette) stitch, ending with a knit row.

SHAPE NECK AND SHOULDERS: beginning with the wrong side facing (to reverse shaping) work from ★ to ★ as for right front.

SLEEVES (TWO THE SAME): Using 4mm (US 6) needles and colour A, cast on 28 (30:32) stitches and work in knit 1, purl 1 rib for 4.5 (4.5:4.5)cm/2 (2:2) in.

above: A simple snowflake pattern is worked in ecru just above the cuffs on each sleeve (see page 127 for chart information).

Increase row: Rib 1 (2:3) stitches ★ increase into the next stitch, rib 4 stitches, repeat from ★ to the last 2 (3:4) stitches, increase into the next stitch, rib 1 (2:3) stitches. *(34: 36:38 stitches)*

Change to 4.5mm (US 7) needles and stocking (stockinette) stitch. Work 4 rows, increasing at each end of row 3 and then work 9 rows of the border pattern (see chart on page 127).

Complete the sleeve in colour A, increasing at each end of every 4th row to 46 (54:62) stitches.

Continue without shaping until the sleeve measures 23 (25:29)cm/9 (10:11^1/2)in. Cast off.

COLLAR: Using 4mm (US 6) needles and colour A cast on 4 stitches. **Row 1 and alternate rows:** knit. **Row 2:** knit 1 stitch, increase into the next 2 stitches, knit 1 stitch *(6 stitches)*. **Row 4:** knit 1, increase into the next stitch, knit 2 stitches, increase into the next stitch, knit 1 stitch. *(8 stitches)*. Continue in this way, increasing at each end of alternate rows to 14 stitches. Now increase 1 stitch at the beginning only of alternate rows to 18 stitches. Knit 76 rows without shaping. Now decrease back down in reverse to 4 stitches. Cast off.

MAKE UP: Weave in all the ends. Lay work out flat, and press each piece gently to flatten out, avoiding the rib trims. Set the sleeves into the armholes, and sew with mattress stitch. Sew the sleeve seams in the same way. Sew the pocket linings down on the inside.

TO FINISH: Sew zipper into position (see page 119). Fold the collar in half lengthways, and pin the centre to the centre of the back of the cardigan. Ease the collar along each side of the neck edge and sew into position. Turn collar down.

left: Thanks to the stranding technique used to create the pattern, this cardigan is exceptionally warm and thick, so it doubles up as a jacket for colder days. This version is knitted in navy and ecru.

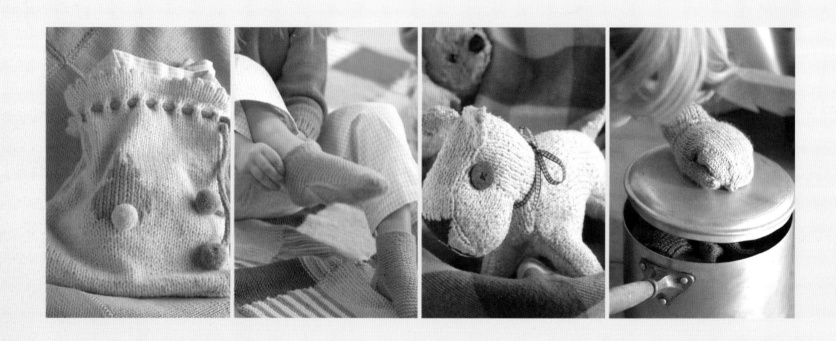

classic accessories

stripy hat

Stripes always look great and this little hat is

perfect to wear with the muffler, or the mittens

on strings, on chilly days. It is worked on two

needles in medium-weight yarn, and takes no

time at all to make. Random colour stripes in

stocking (stockinette) stitch allow you to use

up oddments of wool. The ribbed band gives

the hat a snug fit. If you wish, you could make it

in a plain colour topped with a multi-coloured

pompom (see page 119).

how to make **the stripy hat**

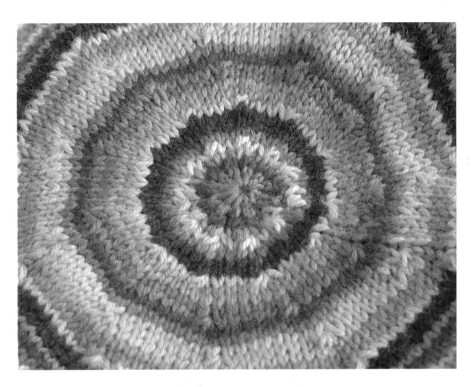

above: The centre of the hat, showing how the colours radiate outwards in random stripes of mixed soft colours.

above right: A contrasting knit 1, purl 1 rib in raspberry makes a neat trim and gives the hat a snug fit.

MATERIALS: Medium-weight yarn (DK yarn) eg Jaeger Matchmaker merino 100 per cent merino wool • Colour A: rain blue: 1 x 50g ball • Colour B: indigo: 1 x 50g ball • Colour C: flannel: 1 x 50g ball • Colour D: seaweed: 1 x 50g ball • Colour E: victoria; 1 x 50g balls • Colour F: oatmeal; 1 x 50g ball • Colour G: raspberry: 1 x 50 g ball • Pair 3.25mm (US 3) needles • Pair 3.75mm (US 5) needles • Coloured yarn for markers • Sewing needle.

HAT SIZE: One size fits all.

STITCH SIZE: This hat has a stitch size of 23 stitches and 32 rows to l0cm (4in) measured over stocking (stockinette) stitch using 3.75mm (US 5) needles.

COLOUR PATTERN: This hat is worked in a 46 row random striped pattern as follows: Colour B: 2 rows; Colour C: 2 rows; Colour D: 1 row; Colour A: 1 row; Colour E: 1 row; Colour D: 1 row; Colour F: 2 rows; Colour A: 1 row: Colour G: 1 row; Colour B: 2 rows; Colour A: 2 rows; Colour C: 3 rows; Colour F: 1 row; Colour G: 1 row; Colour E: 1 row; Colour C: 1 row; Colour B: 2 rows; Colour F: 1 row; Colour C: 2 rows; Colour A: 3 rows; Colour D: 1 row; Colour E: 1 row; Colour D: 1 row; Colour G: 1 row; Colour C: 2 rows; Colour A: 1 row: Colour B: 2 rows: Colour G: 1 row; Colour F: 1 row; Colour C: 1 row; Colour E: 1 row; Colour G: 2 rows.

METHOD: Using 3.25mm (US 3) needles and colour G, cast

on 96 stitches loosely and work in knit 1, purl 1 rib for 8 rows. Change to 3.75mm (US 5) needles. Follow the stripe pattern sequence as given and at the same time shape the hat as follows:

Row 1: knit. **Row 2 and alternative rows:** purl. **Row 3:** knit 8 stitches, ★ increase in next stitch, knit 15 stitches,, repeat from ★ 5 times, increase in the next stitch, knit 7 stitches. *(102 stitches).* **Row 5:** knit 9 stitches, ★increase in the next stitch, knit l6 stitches,repeat from ★ 5 times, increase in the next stitch, knit 7 stitches. *(108 stitches).* Continue to increase in this way on every alternate row until there are 132 stitches. Work 13 rows straight in stocking (stockinette) stitch. **Row 27:** ★knit 3 stitches together, knit 9

stitches, repeat from ★ 11 times. Work 3 rows straight. **Row 31:** ★knit 3 stitches together, knit 7, repeat from ★ 11 times. Continue decreasing in this way on every following 4th row 3 times more. *(22 stitches).* **Row 44:** purl. **Row 45:** knit 1 stitch, ★knit 2 stitches together, repeat from ★ 10 times, knit 1 stitch. **Row 46:** purl.

Break off yarn, thread through remaining stitches, draw up and fasten off.

MAKE UP AND FINISH: Weave in all ends. Lay work out flat, steam gently and press lightly to flatten out, avoiding the rib trims. Join the centre back seam.

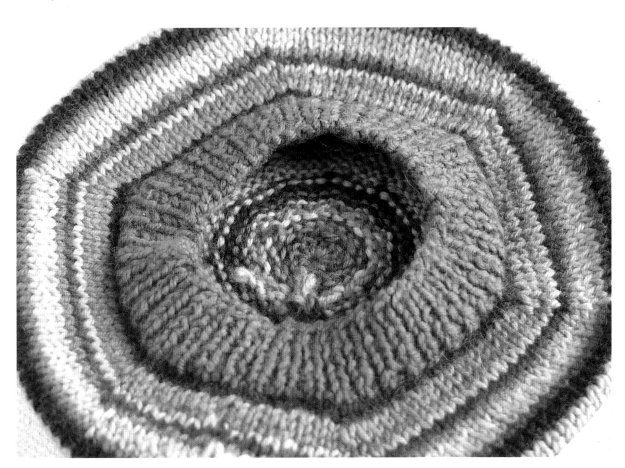

left : The hat makes a neat shape, with approximately 5cm (2in) of random colour rows worked with increases to make the brim.

stripy muffler

Simply effective, this little muffler is worked in stocking (stockinettte) stitch, in fine random stripes. It is a useful piece, as you can use up oddments of yarn for it from other projects. It is worked in one piece, horizontally, providing a modern version of a traditional pattern with the benefit that there are fewer ends to sew in. It is trimmed with an integral garter-stitch edge all round for a neat, flat finish. You can combine it with the mittens and/or the hat to make a matching outfit.

how to make **the stripy muffler**

right: This randomly striped scarf, knitted in stocking (stockinette) stitch, has a neat 4-stitch garter edging all around. It is knitted lengthways, to save tiresome weaving in of ends.

MATERIALS: Medium-weight (DK) yarn, such as Jaeger Matchmaker 100 per cent merino wool• Colour A: rain blue; 1 x 50g ball • Colour B: indigo:1 x 50g ball • Colour C: grey:: 1 x 50g ball • Colour D: seaweed; 1 x 50g ball • Colour E: victoria; 1 x 50g ball • Colour F: oatmeal: 1 x 50g ball • Colour G: raspberry:1 x 50g ball • Pair 4mm (US 6) needles • Sewing needle

SCARF SIZE: This measures 18.5 x 97cm (7^1/4 x 38)in.

STITCH SIZE: This scarf has a stitch size of 22 stitches and 30 rows to 10cm (4in) measured over stocking (stockinette) stitch using 4mm (US 6) needles.

METHOD: The scarf is worked lengthways.
Using 4mm (US 6) needles and colour A, cast on 160 stitches and knit 10 rows.
Change to stocking (stockinette) stitch with 4-stitch garter edgings and work random stripe pattern as follows:
Row 1: using colour A, knit. 4 stitches; using colour B, knit

above : if you wish, you can create different versions of the colour striping. The two above show a primarily raspberry, seaweed, grey and indigo stripe on the left, with a primarily oatmeal, raspberry, grey and indigo stripe on the right.

to the last 4 stitches; using colour A, knit 4 stitches.
Row 2: using colour A, knit 4 stitches; using colour B, purl to the last 4 stitches; using colour A, knit 4 stitches.
Repeat rows 1 and 2 with the following colour changes.
Colour C: 2 rows. Colour D:1 row. Colour A: 1 row. Colour E: 1 row. Colour D: 1 row. Colour F: 2 rows. Colour A: 1 row. Colour G: 1 row. Colour B: 2 rows. Colour A: 2 rows; Colour C: 3 rows, Colour F: 1 row. Colour G: 1 row; Colour E: 1 row; Colour C: 1 row; Colour B: 2 rows; Colour F: 1 row. Colour C: 2 rows. Colour A: 3 rows. Colour D: 1 row. Colour E: 1 row. Colour D: 1 row. Colour G: 1 row.Colour C: 2 rows. Colour A: 1 row. Colour B: 2 rows. Colour G: 1 row. Colour F: 1 row. Colour C: 1 row. Colour E: 1 row. Colour G: 2 rows.
Using colour A, knit 10 rows. Cast off.

TO FINISH: Weave in all the ends.
Lay the work out flat, steam gently and press lightly to flatten out, avoiding the garter stitch trims.

mittens on strings

A little home-made practicality, mittens are a must when the weather gets colder and little hands need to keep warm. The mittens can be made in an evening or on the way to work and back. Knitted in stocking (stockinette) stitch with a rib cuff to tuck up the inside of the coat, they have a little contrasting-colour tip detail. They are designed in two sizes, and you may wish to make several pairs for little gifts for grand-children or nephews and nieces. If you make a little string from tubular knitting to attach to the mittens, and thread them through the sleeves of the coat, the mittens will never stray!

how to make **the mittens on strings**

MATERIALS: Medium-weight yarn e.g. Jaeger Matchmaker 100 per cent merino wool • Colour A: 1 (1) x 50g ball • Colour B: just a scrap • Pair 3mm (US 2) needles • Pair 3.75mm (US 5) needles • 2 small buttons • Sewing needle

SIZING: Two sizes (ages 2-3 and 4-5).

STITCH SIZE: The mittens have a stitch size of 23 stitches and 34 rows to 10cm (4in) measured over stocking (stock-inette) stitch using 3.75mm (US 5) needles.

METHOD: LEFT MITTEN: Using 3mm (US 2) needles and colour B, cast on 36 (38) stitches. Work in knit 1, purl 1 rib for 1 row. Change to colour A and continue in rib for a further 14 rows, increasing 3 (5) stitches evenly over the last row. *(39:43 stitches.)*

Change to 3.75mm (US 5) needles. Work in stocking (stockinette) stitch for 10 rows.

Now divide the stitches for the thumb:

Next row: knit 20 (22) stitches, TURN, cast on 3 stitches.

Next row: purl 11 stitches, TURN, cast on 3 stitches. *(14 stitches).*

Work 8 (10) rows in stocking (stockinette) stitch.

SHAPE TOP: **Row 1:** knit 2 stitches together, ★ knit 1 stitch, knit 2 stitches together, repeat from ★ to the end.

Row 2: purl.

Row 3: ★ knit 2 stitches together, repeat from ★ 3 times, knit 1 stitch.

Break off the yarn, thread the end through a needle and thread through the remaining 5 stitches, draw up and fasten securely.

Join the thumb seam with mattress stitch (see page 120).

PALM: With the right side of the work facing, rejoin colour A to the base of the thumb (at the inner edge of the 12 (14) stitches at right hand side) and pick up and knit 8 stitches from the cast on edge of the thumb, then work across the 19 (21) stitches at the left hand side. *(39:43 stitches).*

Work 15 (17) rows in stocking (stockinette) stitch.

SHAPE TOP: **Row 1:** ★ knit 2 stitches together, knit 2 stitches, repeat from ★ ending with knit 1 stitch (instead of knit 2 stitches. *(29:32 stitches).*

Row 2: purl.

Row 3: knit 2 stitches together, ★ knit 1 stitch, knit 2 stitches together, repeat from ★ to the end. *(19:21 stitches).*

Row 4: purl.

Row 5: knit 3 stitches together. ★ knit 2 stitches together, repeat from ★ to the end. *(9:10 stitches)*

Row 6: purl.

Row 7: (size 2-3): knit 1 stitch, ★ knit 2 stitches together

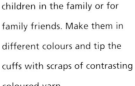

left: Make mittens for all the children in the family or for family friends. Make them in different colours and tip the cuffs with scraps of contrasting coloured yarn.

below: Attach the mittens to each other with a simple knitted rouleau (see page 119). Threaded through the child's coat sleeves, it will ensure the mittens stay together.

across the row; (size 4–5): knit 2 stitches together across the row. *(5 stitches.)*.

Cast off. Break yarn.

Join side seam with an invisible seam.

RIGHT MITTEN: Work as given for the left mitten, to where you "divided for the thumb".

Now divide for the thumb:

Next row: knit 27 (29) stitches, TURN and cast on 3 stitches, TURN.

Next row: purl 11 stitches, TURN, cast on 3 stitches, TURN. *(14 stitches.)*

On these stitches work the thumb as for the left mitten.

PALM: With the right side of he work facing rejoin colour A to the base of the thumb at the inner edge of the 19 (21) stitches at the right hand side, and pick up and knit 8 stitches from the cast on edge of the thumb, then work across the 12 (14) stitches at the left hand side. *(39:43 stitches.)*

Finish as for left mitten

TO FINISH: Make a string as follows:

Using 3.75mm (US 5) needles and colour A, cast on 6 stitches. Every row: ★ knit 1 stitch, yarn forward, slip 1 stitch purlwise, yarn back, repeat from ★ twice. Continue until string measures an appropriate length to thread through two sleeves and across back. **Next row:** ★ knit 2 stitches together, repeat from ★ twice.

Cast off.

Attach each end of the string to the mittens by making a small loop at the end of the string and fastening it to a small button sewn to the inside cuff of each mitten.

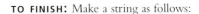

simple socks

Simply knitted on two needles in basic garter stitch, these little socks are very easy and wonderfully quick to make. They have a turned heel and turned-over top. Make several pairs in different colours, as they are always useful and the variations are endless. Use oddments from different projects, tip with contrast or toning colour, or stripe them in multi-colours. They are wonderfully practical as little bed socks for chilly weekends away from home and equally snug in boots. Made in fine merino yarn they would be just as easily knitted in cotton. Or make them in cashmere or alpaca for the ultimate in cosiness.

left: Knitted in fine, warm merino wool, these little socks are wonderfully comfortable, and ideal for wearing around the house or as bedsocks on cold winter nights.

how to make **the simple socks**

MATERIALS: Fine yarn (4 ply yarn) e.g. Jaeger matchmaker merino 100 per cent merino wool • 2 (2:2) x 50g balls • Pair 3mm (US 2) needles • Pair 3.25mm (US 3) needles • Spare needles, safety pins or stitch holder • Sewing needle

SOCK SIZE: Length 9.5 (12:14.5)cm/3$\frac{3}{4}$ (4$\frac{3}{4}$:5$\frac{3}{4}$)in

STITCH SIZE: These socks have a stitch size of 25 stitches and 50 rows to 10cm (4in) measured over garter stitch, using 3.25mm (US 3) needles.

METHOD: (TWO THE SAME): Using 3mm (US 2) needles cast on 31 (34:38) stitches. Work 5 rows in garter stitch, every row knit. Change to 3.25mm (US 3) needles. Knit 26 (30:34) rows. Divide stitches for the heel.

Row 1: knit 9 (9:10) stitches, TURN and slip these stitches onto a spare needle. TURN and knit 14 (16:18) stitches, slip these stitches onto a holder or spare length of yarn for the instep, knit to the end. Knit across the stitches from the spare needle at the beginning of the row.

TURN and work on these 17 (18:20) stitches for the heel. Work 15 rows in stocking (stockinette) stitch, starting with a purl row.

TURN HEEL: **Next row:** knit 9 (10:12) stitches, slip 1 stitch, knit 1 stitch, pass the slipped stitch over, TURN.

Next row: slip 1 stitch purlwise, purl 1 (2:4) stitches, purl 2 stitches together, TURN.

Next row: slip 1 stitch, knit 2 (3:5) stitches, slip 1 stitch, knit 1 stitch, pass the slipped stitch over, TURN.

Next row: slip 1 stitch, purl 3 (4:6) stitches, purl 2 stitches together, TURN.

Continue to work 1 more stitch between the decreases on every row 4 times more. And for the first size only, decrease 1 stitch at the centre of the last row. *(8:10:12 stitches).* Slip the stitches onto a safety pin. Break yarn. Using 3.25mm (US 3) needles and with the right side of the work facing, pick up and knit 10 stitches along the side of the heel, knit across 8 (10:12) stitches on safety pin and pick up and knit 10 stitches along the other side of the heel. *(28:30:32 stitches).* Purl 1 row.

SHAPE SOLE: ★ **Row 1:** knit 1 stitch, slip 1 stitch, knit 1 stitch, pass the slipped stitch over,, knit to the last 3 stitches, knit 2 stitches together, knit 1 stitch.

Row 2: purl. ★

Repeat these 2 rows until 14 (16:18) stitches remain. Work straight until the sole measures 7.5 (10:12.5)cm/3 (4:5)in from the point of the heel (or 2cm/³/₄in less than the total length required), ending with a purl row.

SHAPE TOE: Repeat the 2 rows from ★ to ★ until 6 (8:10) stitches remain.

Slip these stitches onto a safety pin.

INSTEP: Using 3.25mm (US 3) needles, and with the wrong side of the work facing, knit across the 14 (16:18) stitches left on the stitch holder. Continue working in garter stitch until the instep measures the same as the sole (measured from where the stitches were knitted up for the heel to the start of toe shaping), ending with a wrong side row.

FINISH TOE: Repeat the 2 rows from ★ to ★ until 6 (8:10) stitches remain. Slip the stitches from the safety pin onto a needle and graft or cast off the 2 sets of stitches together.

TO FINISH: Weave in all the ends. Steam each sock gently.

left: This side view of the socks shows the garter stitch upper and cuff and the stocking (stockinette) stitch sole and heel, which provide a comfortable base for the sensitive sole of the child's foot.

patched blanket

An essential comforter, this warm and cosy blanket is a new heirloom or "hand me down". Worked in basic garter stitch, in long strips of plain colours and stripes, it is sewn together to make an effective patchwork blanket. It can be edged in fabric prints to coordinate with a child's room, and embroidered with cross stitch to turn it into a special, individual gift. It's a great project for first-time knitters, or one to make collectively for a new arrival. It will do great service as a pram or stroller blanket, and is ideal for afternoon naps or for making a comfy camp.

how to make **the blanket**

MATERIALS: Medium-weight yarn e.g. Rowan wool cotton (50 per cent merino/50 per cent cotton) • Colour A: august: 4 x 50g balls • Colour B: violet: 4 x 50g balls • Colour C: antique: 4 x 50g balls • Colour D: mellow yellow: 4 x 50g balls • Pair 4mm (US 6) needles • Sewing needle •

SIZING: Approximately 90 x 95cm (36 x 38 in).

STITCH SIZE: This blanket has a stitch size of 22 stitches and 30 rows to 10cm (4 in) square measured over stocking (stockinette) stitch, using 4mm (US 6) needles.

TIPS: Yarn: you can work this simple pattern in any yarn, each basic square measures approximately 14 x 18 cm ($5^{1}/_{2}$ x 7 in). It is a simple arithmetical sum to work out how many stitches to cast on and how many rows to knit to make this size.
Personalizing: You may wish to work your personal colourway, style and pattern: the variations are endless.

METHOD: STRIP ONE (MAKE FOUR THE SAME): With colour B, cast on 30 stitches and work in garter stitch (every row knit) in stripes.
★ 4 rows colour B, 4 rows colour C, repeat from ★ 5 more times (48 rows), 4 rows colour B, 52 rows colour D, 52 rows colour A, ★★4 rows colour C, 4 rows colour D. repeat from ★★ 5 times, 4 rows colour C, 52 rows colour A, 52 rows colour D, ★★★4 rows colour B, 4 rows colour C, repeat from ★★★ 5 times,4 rows colour B. Using colour B, cast off.

STRIP TWO (MAKE THREE THE SAME): With colour A, cast on 30 stitches and work in garter stitch stripes as follows. 52 rows colour A, ★4 rows colour D, 4 rows colour B, repeat from ★ 5 times, 4 rows colour D, 52 rows colour C, 52 rows colour B, 52 rows colour C, ★★ 4 rows colour D, 4 rows colour B, repeat from ★★ 5 times, 4 rows colour D, 52 rows colour A. Using colour A cast off.

TO MAKE UP: Weave in all ends and gently press. Using strip 1 for each of the outer edges, sew strips 1 and 2 together alternately, using mattress stitch (see page 119).

OPTIONAL DETAILS: To make a fabric edging for the blanket, cut 7.5cm (3in) wide strips of fabric to the width of the blanket and 2 strips of fabric to the length of the blanket (allowing a little extra for turnings). Fold over the strips of fabric lengthwise and attach to edges of the blanket, butting them together at right angles at the corners.
As an additional decoration, cross stitch over the seams in a contrasting colour.

far left: Made very simply, in garter-stitch squares, this blanket is an ideal size for young children to use when playing or watching television for example, or as a cot or stroller blanket for younger children

above left: The simple pattern consists of plain or striped blocks, knitted in long strips and then seamed together.

right: You can make any choice of colours you like, but one of the most attractive uses harmonizing tones to create a soft, gently unified mixture, as with these mauves, soft yellows and creams. An optional decoration could include cross-stitching over the seam edges, for example, or around particular blocks of colour.

velvet rabbit

The simplest of toys to make and personalize, this little rabbit is knitted in fine velvet-like chenille. It is made in garter stitch in two pieces, and will take only an evening or two to complete. Add character with coloured felt for the eyes and embroidered features, and finish it off with a little pompom tail. For the well-dressed rabbit, make the simplest of frocks from a single piece of linen or gingham, or simply tie a smart cotton-tape bow at the neck. Made in warm, soft colours, this little rabbit is sure to become a firm favourite.

how to make **the velvet rabbit**

right: Coordinating velvet rabbits in black and ecru, one with a taupe velvet bow at the neck, the other with blue and white gingham, are set to play their part in the rabbit's tea party!

MATERIALS: Fine yarn, such as Rowan fine chenille: 1 x 50g ball • Rowan DK cotton or similar yarn for embroidery • Pair 2.75mm (US 1) needles • Narrow tape or gingham ribbon • Scraps of coloured felt • Stuffing • Sewing needle with large eye and spare needle.

RABBIT SIZE: The rabbit measures approximately 36cm (14in) in height.

STITCH SIZE: This rabbit has a stitch size of 28 sttiches and 36 rows to 10cm (4in), measured over garter stitch using 2.75mm (US 1) needles.

BACK: LEG ONE: Using 2.75mm (US 1) needles, cast on 12 stitches and work 36 rows of garter stitch, every row knit. Leave the stitches on a spare needle.

LEG TWO: Cast on 12 stitches and work 36 rows in garter stitch.

Row 37: knit across leg 2, cast on 2 stitches, knit across leg 1. *(26 stitches)*.
Work 79 rows garter stitch, or until the work measures 29cm (11^{1}/2in).

SHAPE EARS: Knit 12 stitches, cast off 2 stitches, knit to the end of the row.
Knit 10 rows.
Next row: decrease 1 stitch (2 stitches in – see page 118) at each end of the row.
Knit 8 rows.
Next row: decrease 1 stitch (2 stitches in) at each end of the row.
Knit 6 rows.
Next row: decrease 1 stitch (2 stitches in) at each end of the row. *(6 stitches.)*.
Knit 2 rows.
Next row: knit 2 stitches, knit 2 stitches together, knit 2 stitches.
Cast off.
Join the yarn to the remaining 12 stitches, and work other ear to match.

FRONT: Make as back.
.
ARMS (TWO THE SAME): Cast on 22 stitches.
Knit 25 rows.
Next row: ★ knit 3 stitches, knit 2 stitches together, repeat from ★ to the last 2 stitches, knit 2 stitches. *(18 stitches)*.
Knit 4 rows.
Next row: ★ knit 2 stitches, knit 2 stitches together, repeat from ★ to the last 2 stitches, knit 2 stitches.
Knit 4 rows.

left: The face of this black rabbit has two white felt eyes, marked with two small blue stitches, and a nose and mouth embroidered in beige. A blue tape bow finishes it off.

below: On this little chocolate-coloured chenille rabbit a pompom tail has been added, made from cream chenille.

Next row: knit 2 stitches, knit 2 stitches together, repeat from ★ to the last 2 stitches, knit 2 stitches *(11 stitches)*.

Knit 2 rows.

Cast off.

Sew cast-on edge to cast-off edge and shaped end of paws.

MAKE UP: Weave in all ends. Lay work out flat and steam each piece gently and press to flatten it out.

Place the back and front of the rabbit together and set in arms approximately 19cm (7$^1/_2$in) from the tip of the ear. Sew on the right side using mattress stitch (see page 119), taking care to include the arms, and leaving an opening large enough to insert the stuffing. Then insert the stuffing, taking care to push it right to the ends of the legs and arms. Close the opening. Sew a line across the neck, to secure.

Cut two little ovals from scraps of felt to make the eyes, and sew them into position.

Embroider a little blue fleck into the corner of each eye.

Embroider the nose and mouth, using simple, long stitches in a contrasting yarn.

Complete with a ribbon bow, tied around the neck.

POMPOM: Make a little pompom for the tail from contrasting yarn, wrapping it over two circles of card (see page 119 for instructions). Stitch the completed pompom to the back of the rabbit, just above the legs.

pyjama bag

This little knitted bag is ideal to keep pyjamas or a nightie cosy and tidy. Items often get scattered around the floor and when bedtime comes it is easier if nightwear is already to hand: a little story and tucking in are then all that is needed. Hang the bag on the door or bedpost. In soft chunky yarn, it is quick and simple to make. A decorative picot edge is threaded with a handmade knitted rouleau and trimmed with little pompoms, which are always good fun to make. The little bunny rabbit embroidered on the front also comes complete with a pompom 'cotton tail'.

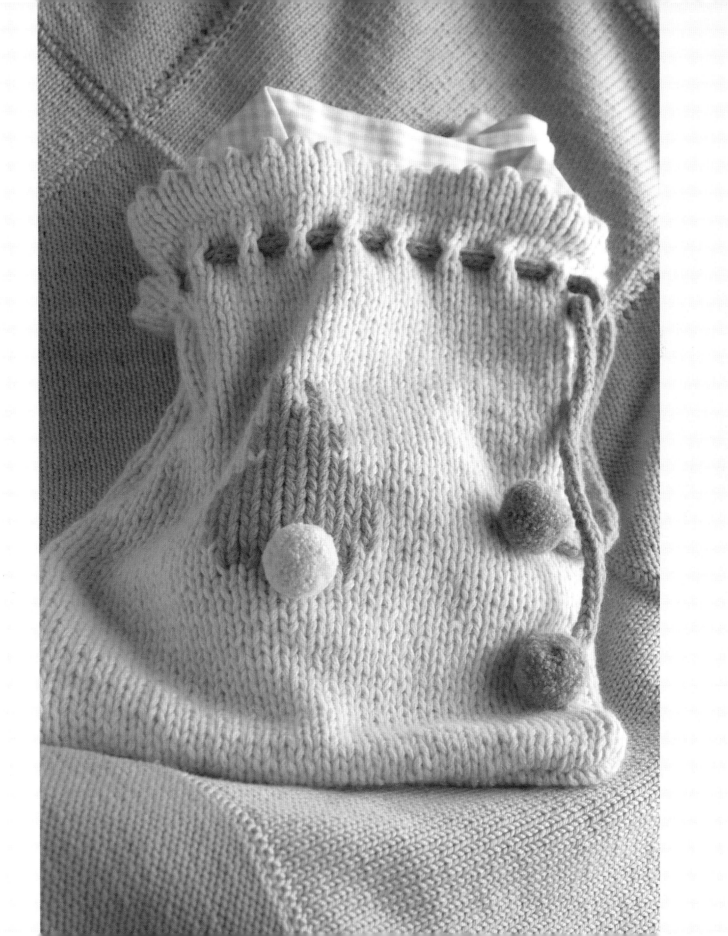

how to make **the pyjama bag**

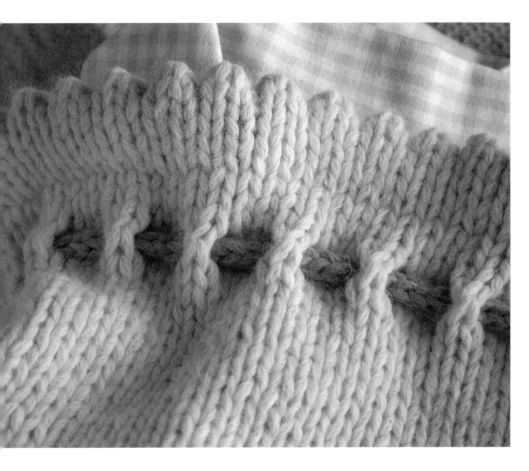

stitch using 6.5mm (US 10^{1}/2) needles.

METHOD: FRONT AND BACK (THE SAME): Using 6.5mm (US 10^{1}/2) needles and colour A, cast on 41 stitches and work 4 rows in stocking (stockinette) stitch.

Next row: knit 1 stitch ★with the yarn forward, knit 2 stitches together, repeat from ★ to the end of the row.

Next row: purl.

Work 4 rows in stocking (stockinette) stitch.

Next row: make the picot hem by knitting together 1 stitch from the needle and 1 loop from the cast-on edge all across the row.

Next row: purl.

Work 2 rows in stocking (stockinette) stitch. Work row of eyelets as follows:

Next row: knit 1 stitch ★with the yarn forward, knit 2 stitches together, repeat from ★ to the end of the row.

Next row: purl.

Continue in stocking (stockinette) stitch until work measures 33cm (13in).

Cast off loosely.

On front only, using colour B, embroider the rabbit motif (see page 126) using Swiss darning stitch (see page 119).

MAKING A POMPOM: Cut out two cardboard circles approximately 4 cm (1^{1}/2in) in diameter and cut a hole carefully in the centre of each. Hold the two circles together and using the colour of your choice, wound into a ball small enough to pass through the centre of the hole, take the yarn from the centre to the edge of the card and back, keeping the strands close together. Work as many layers as possible before the centre hole becomes too small

above: The top of the bag has a picot-edged hem as a pretty finishing detail, with a rouleau string threaded through just below it.

MATERIALS: Chunky weight yarn eg Jaeger Chamonix (angora/merino/polyamide) • Colour A: 2 x 50g balls • Colour B: 1 x 50g ball • Pair 6.5 mm (US 10^{1}/2) needles • Pair 4 mm (US 6) double-pointed needles • Large-eyed sewing needle

SIZE: Length 33cm (13in); width 25.5cm (10in).

STITCH SIZE: This bag has a stitch size of 16 stitches and 18 rows to 10cm (4in) measured over stocking (stockinette)

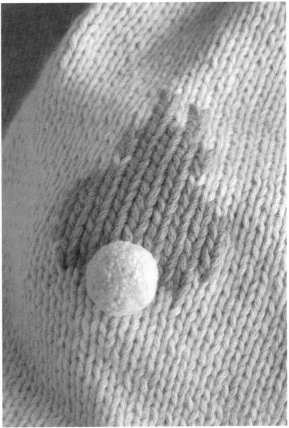

far left: Draw the bag up by means of the knitted rouleau string, which has a pompom finishing touch at each end.

left: The decorative rabbit detail on the front of the bag has a little pompom tail as an additional adornment.

for the ball of yarn to pass through. Using sharp scissors, slip one of the blades between the two layers of card and cut around the circumference of the circle. Slip a length of yarn between the two layers and around the centre of what will become a pompon. Pull tight and knot the yarn, and cut away the card. Shake, fluff up and trim the pompom to shape (see also page 119).

MAKING A ROULEAU: This is a very quick and easy method of making a string. Using 4mm (US 6) double-pointed needles, and the required yarn, cast on 3 stitches and knit 3 stitches. Do not turn the work; slide the stitches to the right tip of the needle again and knit them, pulling the yarn across from the right, to create a tube of knitting to the required length (see also page 119).

TO FINISH: Weave in all ends. Join side seams and bottom edge. Sew pompon on rabbit for tail. Thread rouleau through eyelet holes and trim with two pompons. Draw up the top of the bag.

top dog

A nostalgic look back at childhood is not complete without a reminder of our favourite pet. Mine was Topper, a dizzy wire-haired fox terrier. This one is a little less excitable! Knitted in a slubby chunky-weight textured yarn in basic stocking (stockinette) stitch, it is worked from the tail to the head, increasing and decreasing to create a simple shape. His ears and tail are added afterwards and a smart black and white gingham ribbon around his neck ensures he looks well turned out. Try other textures like tweeds and boucles for different effects; don't worry too much about the tension or stitch size: he will just come out a little smaller or larger.

left: These are a selection of the materials you will need to create your toy dog. The eyes and nose are simply circles and a triangle respectively, cut from charcoal felt, and suitably embroidered.

right: The head of this toy dog is endearingly large, giving it a cuddly appearance. A smart black and white gingham bow around his neck adds a debonair touch.

how to make **the top dog**

MATERIALS: Chunky weight texture yarn e.g. Rowan Summer Tweed • 2 x 50g balls • Pair 3.75mm • (US 5) needles • Spare needles • Gingham ribbon • Stuffing • Embroidery thread • Large sewing needle • Charcoal felt for nose and eyes • Scissors

SIZE: Height (to top of head): 21cm (8¼in) • Width (from nose to tail): 30cm (12in).

STITCH SIZE: This dog has a stitch size of 22 stitches and 30 rows to 10cm (4in) measured over stocking (stockinette) stitch, using 3.75mm (US 5) needles.

METHOD: BACK LEG **1:** Using 3.75mm (US 5) needles cast on 6 stitches, and work in stocking (stockinette) stitch as follows:
Row 1: knit. **Row 2:** purl. **Row 3:** cast on 7 stitches, knit *(13 stitches)*. **Row 4:** purl. **Row 5:** cast on 7 stitches, knit *(20 stitches)*. **Row 6:** purl. **Row 7:** cast on 7 stitches, knit *(27 stitches)*. **Row 8:** cast off 2 stitches, purl. Cut the yarn.
Leave this work on a spare needle.

BACK LEG **2:** Cast on 6 stitches. **Row 1:** knit. **Row 2:** cast on 7 stitches, purl *(13 stitches)*. **Row 3:** knit. **Row 4:** cast on 7 stitches, purl *(20 stitches)*.

Row 5: knit. **Row 6:** cast on 7 stitches, purl *(27 stitches)*. **Row 7:** cast off 2 stitches, knit *(25 stitches)*. **Row 8:** cast on 3 stitches, purl *(28 stitches)*.

BODY: **Row 9:** knit 2 stitches together, knit across back leg 2, cast on 9 stitches, knit across back leg 1 to the last 2 stitches, knit 2 stitches together *(60 stitches)*. **Rows 10-25:** decrease 1 stitch at each end of every row to 28 stitches. **Row 26:** purl. **Rows 27-40:** now increase 1 stitch at each end of the next and every alternate row to 42 stitches. **Rows 41-42:** increase 1 stitch at each end of each row *(46 stitches)*. **Rows 43-44:** cast on 4 stitches at the beginning of the next 2 rows *(54 stitches)*. **Row 45:** cast on 5 stitches, knit. **Row 46:** cast on 5 stitches, purl 30 stitches, cast off 4 stitches, purl to the end.
Working on the last 30 stitches, shape neck.
Row 47: cast on 2 stitches, knit to the last 2 stitches, knit 2 stitches together *(31 stitches)*. **Rows 48-52:** decrease 1 stitch at the neck edge on every row to 26 stitches. **Row 53:** cast off 13 stitches, knit to the last 2 stitches, knit 2 stitches together *(12 stitches)*. **Row 54:** purl 2 stitches together, purl to the end of the row. **Row 55:** cast off 4 stitches, knit to the last 2 stitches, knit 2 stitches together *(6 stitches)*. **Row 56:** purl. **Row 57:** cast off 4 stitches, knit to end *(2 stitches)*. **Row 58:** cast off .
With right sides facing, rejoin yarn to remaining stitches.
Row 47: knit 2 stitches together, knit to the end *(29 stitches)*. **Row 48:** cast on 2 stitches, purl to the last 2 stitches, purl 2 together *(30 stitches)*. **Row 49-53:** decrease 1 stitch at the neck edge on every row *(25 stitches)*. **Row 54:** cast off 13 stitches, purl to last 2 stitches, purl 2 stitches together *(11 stitches)*. **Row 55:** knit 2 stitches together, knit to end. **Row 56:** cast off 4 stitches, purl to the last 2 stitches, purl 2 stitches together *(5 stitches)*. **Row 57:** knit. **Row 58:** cast off 3 stitches, purl to end *(2 stitches)*. **Row 59:** cast off.

HEAD: With right side of work facing pick up and knit 28 stitches evenly around the neck shaping. **Row 1:** purl. **Row 2:** knit. **Row 3:** decrease 1 stitch at each end *(26 stitches)*. **Row 4:** knit. **Row 5:** decrease 1 stitch at each end *(24 stitches)*. **Rows 6-24:** work in stocking (stockinette) stitch as set but marking row 13 at each end with with coloured thread. **Row 25:** purl 11 stitches, cast off 2 stitches, purl to the end.
Working on the last 11 stitches: **Row 26:** knit. **Row 27:** purl 2 stitches together, purl to the end. **Row 28:** cast off 5 stitches, knit to the end. **Row 29:** purl. **Row 30:** cast off.
Rejoin yarn to the remaining stitches.
Row 26: knit to the end of the row. **Row 27:** cast off 5 stitches, purl to the last 2 stitches, purl 2 stitches together. **Row 28:** knit. **Row 29:** cast off.

LEFT MUZZLE: With the right side facing, pick up and knit 14 stitches between head cast off and marker:
Row 1: purl. **Row 2:** knit. **Row 3:** cast on 3 stitches, purl to the end. **Row 4:** knit 2 stitches together, knit to the end. **Row 5:** cast on 2 stitches, purl to the end. **Row 6:** knit. **Row 7:** purl to the last 2 stitches, purl 2 stitches together **Row 8:** knit. **Row 9:** purl. **Row 10:** knit 2 stitches together, knit to the end. **Row 11:** cast off 4 stitches, purl to the end. **Row 12:** knit 2 stitches together, knit to the end. **Row 13:** cast off 3 stitches, purl to the end. **Row 14:** cast off.

RIGHT MUZZLE: With right side facing, pick up and knit 14 stitches between marker and head cast off.. **Row 1:** purl. **Row 2:** cast on 3 stitches, knit to the end. **Row 3:** purl 2 stitches together, purl to the end. **Row 4:** cast on 2 stitches, knit to the end. *(18 stitches)*. **Row 5:** purl. **Row 6:** knit to the last 2 stitches, knit 2 stitches together. **Row 7:** purl. **Row 8:** knit. **Row 9:** purl 2 stitches together, purl to the end. **Row 10:** cast off 4 stitches, knit to the end. **Row 11:** purl 2 stitches together, purl to the end. **Row 12:** cast off 3 stitches, knit to the end. **Row 13:** cast off.

BODY GUSSET: Cast on 2 sttiches. **Row 1:** purl. **Row 2:** increase in each stitch. **Row 3:** purl. **Rows 4-13:** increase at each end of next and alternate rows *(14 stitches)*. **Rows 14-15:** stocking (stockinette) stitch. **Rows 16-17:** cast on l6 stitches at the beginning of row *(46 stitches)*. **Rows 18-24:** stocking (stockinette) stitch. **Row 25:** decrease 1 stitch at each end of row *(44 stitches)*. **Rows 26-33:** cast off 3 stitches at the beginning of every row *(20 stitches)*. **Rows 34-38:** decrease 1 stitch at each end of every row *(10 stitches)*. **Row 39:** increase 1 stitch at each end of row. **Rows 40-54:** increase 1 stitch at each end of rows 41, 44, 47, 50 and 53 *(22 stitches)*. **Rows 55-63:** increase 1 stitch at each end of every row *(40 stitches)*. **Rows 64-69:** work without shaping. **Row 70:** cast off.

HEAD GUSSET: Cast on 2 stitches. **Row 1:** purl. **Row 2:** increase in first stitch, knit 1 stitch. **Row 3:** purl. **Rows 4-10:** work in stocking (stockinette) stitch, increasing at each end of next and alternate rows *(11 stitches)*. **Rows 11-80:** stocking (stockinette) stitch. **Rows 81-83:** decrease 1 stitch at each end of every row *(5 stitches)*. **Row 84:** cast off.

EARS (MAKE FOUR): Cast on 8 stitches and work in stocking (stockinette) stitch, decreasing 1 stitch at each end

above: The head of the toy dog is knitted in three parts: a left muzzle, a right muzzle and head gusset, which forms the face of the dog, onto which the nose and mouth are stitched.

of rows 5, 8 and 11. **Row 12:** purl 2 stitches together. Fasten off.

TAIL: Cast on 13 stitches and work in stocking (stockinette) stitch, decreasing 1 stitch each end of rows 4, 7, 10, 13 and 15. Purl 1 row. Cast off.

TO MAKE UP: Weave in all the ends. Lay work out flat and steam each piece lightly to flatten.

1 Fold legs and body in half along the centre, mark centre at back legs.

2 Insert the head gusset, with the pointed part at the top of the head and the blunt part under the chin and neck. Ease the gusset length around the head shape, making sure to square up shapings on head to give characteristic shape. Back-stitch into position.

3 With right sides facing, pin body gusset to legs and back, matching legs and gusset cast-on to the centre back legs marker, easing shapings between front and back legs. Backstitch all around, leaving a gap for stuffing. Turn right side out and stuff, taking care with all the little areas. Close gap.

4 Fold the tail in half lengthways and stitch the long side. Turn right sides out and attach to the dog.

5 Sew two ears together, wrong sides facing. Repeat for second ear. Attach each to the top of the head.

6 Sew buttons or felt shapes for the eyes and a triangle for the nose. Make the mouth by working two lines of embroidery from either side of the nose to the tip.

useful information

erika's tips

This book is simple in its concept, designs and ideas, but introduces some tips and techniques, collected over the years, to make that little bit of a difference.

READING PATTERNS: Always read the pattern through carefully before starting the work. The patterns do not use many abbreviations – I prefer to use the term in full as abbreviations are very off putting for the new knitter and can be misinterpreted, causing confusion.

WORKING FROM A CHART: Designs with two or more colours are worked from a chart (see pages 126-7) and the colours are indicated by symbols. Each square represents a stitch and each row of squares represents a row of knitting. The patterns are worked in stocking (stockinette) stitch (one row knit, one row purl), unless otherwise stated. Read the knit rows from right to left and the purl rows from left to right.

WORKING WITH COLOURS:

There are three ways of working with colour:

STRANDING OR FAIRISLE: Work with each colour according to the sequence from the chart, letting the colour not in use strand itself loosely all across the back of the fabric. It is usual to strand the yarn across the back every 3 stitches, but doing it every stitch gives a much neater appearance and minimizes the risk of a little hand getting caught up on the finished garment. Take care not to pull too tightly as this will "ruckle" the work.

SWISS DARNING (DUPLICATE STITCH): This is a very simple method of applying coloured patterns to a finished garment. Use it instead of stranding as a quicker, easier and neater method, as it leaves you to concentrate on the knitting. It is especially useful where there are single-coloured stitches.

The Swiss-darned stitch is worked on top of the knitted stocking (stockinette) stitches in a contrast colour. Using a blunt-ended sewing needle and the yarn of choice, simply duplicate the shape of the V-stitch, starting at the back of the work.

COLOUR BLOCKS : When working large areas of colour, use separate pieces or balls of yarn for each new colour change, twisting strands of yarn at the back of work to avoid a hole.

JOINING IN NEW YARNS: Join in a new ball of yarn at the beginning of a row (never in the middle), weaving the "tail" in as you knit. To calculate if you have sufficient yarn to finish a row, simply spread out the yarn along the width of the knitting, back and forth three times; this will give sufficient yarn to finish the row.

FULLY FASHIONED INCREASES AND DECREASES: A personal "twist", or trade mark, of mine is to work the increases and decreases 2 or 3 stitches in from the edge of the garment. This gives a fully fashioned detail which enhances essentially plain or simple garments, and is especially attractive around necklines and armholes.

INTREGAL KNITTING: Many of the designs have trims and details worked integrally; this always looks neater and is quicker, as well as minimizing sewing up at the end. Knit in pocket tops where possible. It is much neater and easier than lining them up and avoids he pocket top "pulling".

Work the edging for a V-neck in at the same time as the body of the knitting: this looks neat, and is very easy to do. When working on each set of stitches either side of the neck shaping, simply work the first few stitches bordering the V, in rib: knit 1 stitch, purl 1 stitch. This is shown in the classic long-sleeved jumper on page 18.

A useful quick tip is to work the two sleeves at the same time, on the same needle, using a separate ball of yarn for each.

Work the buttonbands in with the fronts to give a neater finish, a better edge and a better fit. It also saves having to pick up stitches!

ALTERNATIVE EDGINGS

PICOT EDGE: This provides a very sweet alternative to traditional edgings, especially for very simple designs, such as the denim pinafore, and adds a little "feminity" to a robust yarn.

TUBULAR HEM: This holds the garment straight and boxy. Use it to change the appearance of a design you may have knitted time after time.

RIB WELT: This is the classic edge to most garments. Owing to its elasticity, it is both a functional and decorative stitch, pulling in or gripping at the

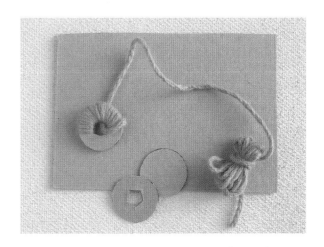

left: Knitted rouleau strings are quick and easy to make on a pair of double-pointed needles. Instructions are given below.

right: Little pompoms make a neat decorative finish to rouleau strings and to the rabbit design on the pyjama bag. Instructions are given below.

bottom of the garment and trimming necks and armholes. Vary with different rib combinations, such as knit 2, pearl 2, or uneven numbers, such as knit 3, purl 1, for a different effect.

BUTTONHOLES: Information on how to wo rk buttonholes is given in the relevant patterns.

EMBROIDERY: I have used very simple embroidery in projects such as the short sleeve jumper, to "ring the changes". It is basic stem and satin stitch.

FINISHING OFF: Sew in ends, using a blunt needle. "Weave" each end separately across the fabric of the work on the wrong side (never along the edges, as this makes it very bulky to sew up, especially important in projects using garter stitch, such as the blanket) for about 4 stitches, then back 1 or 2 stitches to hold it firmly in place.

MAKING A ROULEUAU: This is a very quick and easy method of making a string. You will need two double-pointed needles, and the required yarn. Cast on 3 stitches and knit. Do not turn; instead slide the stitches to the right tip of the needle again and knit them, pulling the yarn across from the right, firmly, in this way, you create knitted tube. You simple use the knit stitch repeat until the rouleau is the required length.

MAKING A POMPOM: Cut out two cardboard circles approximately 4cm (1^1/2in) in diameter and cut identical holes in the centre of each. Hold the

two circles together and, using the colour of your choice wound into a ball small enough to pass through the centre of the hole, pull the ball through the centre hold, winding the yarn over the circles, keeping the strands close together. Work as many layers as you can before the centre hole becomes too small for the ball of yarn to pass through. Using sharp scissors, slip one of the blades between the two outer layers of card and cut around the circumference of the circle. Slip a length of yarn between the two layers and around the centre of what will become the pompon Pull tight and knot the yarn. Cut away the card, shake, fluff up and trim the pompon to shape.

RIBBON: Add ribbon to the buttonbands of cardigans, to give a decorative twist or sew it on the outside of the cardigan and attach the buttons to it. Seams were traditionally taped along the shoulders to keep them in position, and this technique is still employed in many couture garments. I have used a very fine gingham ribbon, applied to the back neck and inside shoulder seams to add a little personal touch.

ZIPPERS: Pin the zipper to the opening, being sure that the knitting fits easily and is neither ruckled or stretched. The knitted edges should come right up to the teeth of the zipper. Work in back stitch along the edges using a sewing thread. Be sure to choose a zipper that is the correct weight for the garment and, of course, open-ended.

SEAMS: MATTRESS STITCH (OR INVISIBLE STITCH) This is used to join all side and sleeve seams or where a flat seam with no bulk is required. The real beauty of the stitch is that is worked from the right side so you can always see where you are going. With the right side of both pieces facing, secure the yarn to the edge of one piece. Take a blunt-ended, large-eyed needle across to the opposite edge, pick up the equivalent stitch on this piece, pull the yarn through; take the needle back to the first edge, returning the needle through the hole of the previous a stitch and pull the yarn through.

BACKSTITCH SEAM: This is used where a firm edge is required to hold the shape, such as a set in sleeve or to give strength at any point where the garment may take extra strain. Place the pieces together, right sides facing. Work along the wrong side of the fabric, one stitch from the edge. Secure the yarn and work from right to left. With the needle at the back of the work, move along to the left, the length of one knitted stitch, bring the needle through, take the needle from left to right across the front of the work, to the end of the last stitch, put the needle through the fabric to the back of the work, pull the yarn through. Repeat for the required length. Fasten yarn off neatly on the wrong side of the work.

SLIP STITCH: This is used to secure tubular hems or picot trims, for example. Simply stitch along the wrong side of the fabric one stitch from the edge. Secure the yarn and work from right to left. With the needle at the back of the work move it along to the left, the length of one knitted stitch, bring the needle through, take the needle from left to right across the front of the work, to end of the last stitch, put the needle through the fabric to the back of the work, pull the yarn through.

KNITTING TERMS:

SLIP THE FIRST STITCH: Transfer the sttich from the left needle to the right needle without knitting it.

THROUGH THE BACK LOOPS: Put the right needle through the back loops of the next two stitches and knit or pearl them as though they were one stitch. On a purl row, this takes a little practice.

YARN FORWARD: Used to make a 'hole'. Bring the yarn forward as if to purl the stitch, take it back over the right needle, and then work the next instruction in the usual way.

YARN OVER: Used to make a 'hole'. Take yarn over the right needle, from front to back of the work, and then under the right needle to the front of the work, and then work as for the next instruction.

SPECIAL YARN TIPS:

COTTON: If you have been working with wool for a long time, you need to tension cotton differently, a little tighter maybe, so go down a needle size, being particularly careful on the outside stitch.

CHENILLE: If the yarn used in the rabbit design is cotton, it has little or no give, so you may need to go down a needle size, as he needs to be made firm, especially over garter stitch. However, he is perfect in chenille and well worth the effort!

Do not attempt to sew with chenille as it will shed: instead chose a yarn of similar colour (wool or cotton is best) and sew using back stitch.

CARE OF KNITTING AND YARNS

KEEPING WORK CLEAN: To keep your work clean, especially when working in light colours, k eep the knitting in a bag or a pillowslip when not in use. Always wash your hands before knitting with pale yarns. If your hands or the yarn feel "sticky", use talcum powder.

WASHING AND CARE: Check the ball-bands of the yarns you use for washing instructions. Most of those suggested in this book can be machine washed at cool temperatures and lightly spun dried. Luxury yarns such as angora will need to be hand-washed at cool temperatures, rinsed well, squeezed gently between towels and dried flat.

Pressing should be done with a steam iron (or over a damp cloth).

Any stains are best treated while still wet by soaking the garment in cold water. Proprietary stain removers can be applied (check colour fastness first on a less visible part of the garmet) and the garment can then be washed in the usual way.

substituting yarns

If you can, it is always best to use the yarn recommended in the knitting pattern (see pages 123-5 for suppliers). However, if you do decide to use an alternative yarn, be sure to purchase a substitute yarn that is as close as possible to the original in thickness, weight and texture so that it will be compatible with the knitting instructions given in each of the patterns in this book. Calculate quantities required by the lengths given the rather than by ball weights, and buy only one ball to start with, so that you can test the effect and the tension to avoid disappointment and unnecessary expense.

If using an alternative or substitute yarn, the most important factor is matching the tension specified by the pattern. (Refer to pages 10-11 for information on tension).

Remember that once you have selected the alternative yarn you must be sure that you have enough yarn to complete the garment or project, as the number of metres (yards) on the ball of the substitute yarn may be different from the original.

YARNS USED

The following is a list of the yarns used for projects in this book. The yarn characteristics are helpful if you are trying to find an alternative yarn.

Note: the tensions given are all measured over stocking (stockinette) stitch and the ball/hank lengths are approximate.

All yarns can be hand washed or dry cleaned (in certain solvents). Those marked with a ★ can be machine washed.

FINE YARNS

These generally knit to a 4 ply weight.

Jaeger Matchmaker merino 4 ply: a 4 ply wool yarn; 100 per cent merino wool. Approx 183m (200yd) per 50g ball.
Recommended tension is 28 stitches and 36 rows to 10cm (4in) using 3.75mm (US 3) needles.

★Jaeger baby merino 4 ply: a 4 ply wool yarn; 100 per cent merino. Approx 183m (200yd) per 50g ball.
Recommended tension is 28 stitches and 36 rows to 10cm (4in) using 3.75mm (US 3) needles.

Rowan 4 ply soft: a 4 ply wool yarn; 100 per cent merino wool. Approx 175m (191yd) per 50g ball
Recommended tension is 28 stitches and 36 rows to 10cm (4in) using 3.75mm (US 3) needles.

★Rowan 4 ply cotton: a matt 4 ply cotton yarn; 100 per cent pure cotton. Approx 170m (185yd) per 50g ball
Recommended tension is 27-29 stitches and 37-39 rows to 10cm (4in) using 3 to 3.75 mm (US 2 to 3) needles.

Rowan lurex shimmer: a 4 ply metallic yarn; 80 per cent viscose, 20 per cent polyester. Approx 95m (104yd) per 50g ball
Recommended tension is 29 stitches and 41 rows to 10cm (4in) using 3.75mm (US 3) needles.

Jaeger silk: a 4 ply silk yarn; 100 per cent silk. Approx 186 m (201yd) per 50g ball.
Recommended tension is 28 stitches and 38 rows to 10cm (4in) using 3mm (US 3) needles.

Jaeger Cashmina: a 4 ply luxury blend yarn; 80 per cent cashmere/20 per cent extra fine merino. Approx 125m (136yd) per 50 g ball.
Recommended tension is 28 stitches and 38 rows to 10cm (4in) using 3.75mm (US 3) needles.

Rowan fine cotton chenille: a 4 ply cotton yarn –89 per cent cotton, 11 per cent polyester. Approx 160m (175yd) per 50g ball.
Recommended tension is 20-25 stitches and 36-44 rows to 10cm (4in) using 2 75 to 3mm (US 2 to 3) needles.

MEDIUM YARNS

These generally knit to a double knit weight.

*Rowan wool cotton: a double knitting weight blend yarn, 50 per cent merino/50 per cent cotton. Approx 113 m (123yd) per 50g ball. Recommended tension is 22-24 stitches and 30-32 rows to 10cm (4in) using 3.75 to 4mm (US 5 to 6) needles.

*Rowan denim: a double knitting weight yarn, 100 per cent pure cotton. Approx 93 m (102yd) per 50g ball.
Recommended tension is 20 stitches and 28 rows to 10cm (4in) using 4 mm (US 6) needles.

*Rowan handknit DK cotton, 100 per cent pure cotton. Approx 85m (93yd) per 50g ball.
Recommended tension is 9-20 stitches and 28 rows to 10cm (4in) using 4 to 4.5mm (US 6 to 7) needles.

*Jaeger Matchmaker merino DK: a double knitting weight yarn, 100 per cent merino wool. Approx 120m (131yd) per 50g ball.
Recommended tension is 22 stitches and 30 rows to 10cm (4in) using 4mm (US 6) needles.

*Jaeger baby merino DK: a double knitting weight blend yarn, 100 per cent merino wool. Approx 120m (131yd) per 50g ball.
Recommended tension is 22 stitches and 30 rows to 10cm (4in) using 4mm (US 6) needles.

Jaeger mohair art: a double knitting weight blend yarn, 50 per cent mohair/50 per cent nylon. Approx 113m (123 yd) per 50g ball.
Recommended tension is 22-24 stitches and 30-32 rows to 10cm (4in) using 3.75 to 4mm (US 5 to 6) needles.

CHUNKY YARNS

These generally knit to an Aran weight.

*Jaeger Matchmaker Merino Aran: a double knitting weight yarn, 100 per cent merino wool. Approx 82m (90yd) per 50g ball.
Recommended tension is 19 stitches and 25 rows to 10cm (4in) using 4.5mm (US 7) needles.

Jaeger Chamonix: a chunky knitting weight blend yarn, 48 per cent angora, 47 per cent extra fine merino, 5 per cent polyamide. Approx 110m (120yd) per 50g ball.
Recommended tension is 14 stitches and 20 rows 10cm (4in) using 7mm (US 10 to 11) needles.

*Rowan all seasons cotton: a chunky weight yarn, 60 per cent cotton/40 acrylic/microfibre. Approx 90m (98yd) per 50g ball.
Recommended tension is 16-18 stitches and 23-25 rows to 10cm (4in) using 4.5 to 5.5mm (US 7 to 9) needles.

Rowan summer tweed: a chunky weight slubby silk cotton blend yarn. 70 per cent silk /30 per cent cotton. Approx 108m (118yd) per 50g ball.
Recommended tension is 16 stitches and 23 rows to 10cm (4in) using 5mm (US 9) needles.

suppliers

SELECTED ROWAN STOCKISTS

See previous pages for information about the Rowan yarns used in this book. To obtain Rowan yarns, look below to find a distributor or store in your area. To find the most up-to-date list of stores near you selling Rowan yarns, contact Rowan head office in England or the Rowan website.

ROWAN YARNS WEBSITE

Website: www.knitrowan.com

Rowan, Green Lane Mill, Holmfirth, West Yorkshire HD9 2DX, England.
Telephone: + 44 (0) 1484 681 881.
Fax: + 44 (0) 1484 687 920.

AVON

BATH – Rowan at Stitch Shop,
15 The Podium, Northgate.
Mail order.
Tel: 01225 481134.
BRISTOL – Rowan at John Lewis,
Cribbs Causeway. Mail order.
Tel: 0117 959 1100.
Rowan at House of Fraser,
The Horsefair. Mail order.
Tel: 0117 944 5566.
STAPLE HILL – Knitting Well,
105 High Street. Tel: 0117 970 1740.

BEDFORDSHIRE

LEIGHTON BUZZARD – Rowan at Needle & Thread, 2/3 Peacock Mews.
Mail order.
Tel: 01525 376456.
LUTON – Kaytes Needlecrafts,
4 The Gallery, Arndale Centre.
Tel: 01582 482517.

BERKSHIRE

READING – Rowan at John Lewis, Broad Street. Mail order.
Tel: 01189 575955.
WINDSOR – W J Daniels & Co Ltd, 120–125 Peascod Street. Mail order.
Tel: 01753 862106. E-mail: enquiry@danielstores.co.uk

BUCKINGHAMSHIRE

MILTON KEYNES – Rowan at John Lewis, Central Milton Keynes.
Mail order. Tel: 01908 679171.

CAMBRIDGESHIRE

CAMBRIDGE – Rowan at Robert Sayle, St Andrews Street.
Mail order. Tel: 01223 361292.
PETERBOROUGH – John Lewis, Queensgate Centre. Mail order.
Tel: 01733 344644.

CHESHIRE

CHEADLE – Rowan at John Lewis, Wilmslow Road. Mail order.
Tel: 0161 491 4914.

CORNWALL

PENZANCE – Iriss, 66 Chapel Street.
Mail order. Tel: 01736 366568.
E-mail: iriss@penzance.ws
Website: http://penzance.ws
TRURO – Rowan at Truro Fabrics, 105/106 Kenwyn Street. Mail order.
Tel: 01872 222130.
Website: www.trurofabrics.com
WADEBRIDGE – Rowan at Artycrafts, 41 Molesworth Street. Mail order.
Tel: 01208 812274. E-mail: artycrafts@ukonline.co.uk

COUNTY DURHAM

DARLINGTON – Rowan at Binns,
7 High Row. Mail order.
Tel: 01325 462606.

CUMBRIA

BRAMPTON – The Bobbin Box, Unit 2 Old George, Market Place.
Tel: 01697 73611.
PENRITH – Rowan at Indigo, 1 St Andrews View. Mail order.
Tel: 01768 899917.
E-mail: carolyn@indigoknits.co.uk
Website: www.indigoknits.co.uk
PENRITH – Just Sew, Poet Walk. Tel: 01768 866791.

DEVON

BIDEFORD – Wool and Needlecraft Shop, 49 Mill Street. Tel: 01237 473015.
EXETER – Inspirations, 7 Piazza Terracina, Haven Road. Mail order.
Tel: 01392 435115.
PLYMOUTH – Rowan at Dingles, 40–46 Royal Parade. Mail order.
Tel: 01752 266611.
TOTNES – Sally Carr Designs, The Yarn Shop, 31 High Street. Tel: 01803 863060.

DORSET

CHRISTCHURCH – Honora, 69 High Street. Tel: 01202 486000.
Website: www.knittingyarns.co.uk
DORCHESTER – Goulds Ltd, 22 South Street. Tel: 01305 217816.
SHERBORNE – Hunters of Sherborne, 4 Tilton Court, Digby Road.
Tel: 01935 817722.
SWANAGE – The Wool & Craft Shop, 17 Station Road. Tel: 01929 422814.
WIMBORNE – Rowan at The Walnut Tree, 1 West Borough. Tel: 01202 840722.

ESSEX

CHELMSFORD – Franklins, 219 Moulsham Street. Tel: 01245 346300.
COLCHESTER – Franklins, 13/15 St Botolphs Street.
Tel: 01206 563955.
MALDON – Peachey Ethknits, 6/7 Edwards Walk. Mail order.
Tel: 01621 857102.
E-mail: ethknits@ethknits.co.uk

Website: www.ethknits.co.uk
SOUTHEND-ON-SEA – Gades, 239 Churchill South, Victoria Circus.
Tel: 01702 613789.

GLOUCESTERSHIRE

CHELTENHAM – Rowan at Cavendish House, The Promenade. Mail order.
Tel: 01242 521300.
CIRENCESTER – Ashley's Wool Specialist, 62 Dyer Street. Mail order.
Tel: 01285 653245.

GREATER MANCHESTER

DIDSBURY – Rowan at Sew In of Didsbury, 741 Wilmslow Road.
Tel: 0161 4455861.
E-mail: enquiries@knitting-and-needle-work.co.uk
Website: www.knitting-and-needlework.co.uk
MARPLE – Rowan at Sew In of Marple, 46 Market Street. Tel: 0161 427 2529.
E-mail: enqiries@knitting-and-needle-work.co.uk Website: www.knitting-and-needlework.co.uk

HAMPSHIRE

BASINGSTOKE – Pack Lane Wool Shop, 171 Pack Lane, Kempshott.
Tel: 01256 323644.
LYMINGTON – Leigh's, 56 High Street.
Tel: 01590 673254.
NEW MILTON – Smith Bradbeer & Co Ltd, 126–134 Station Road.
Tel: 01425 613333.
SOUTHAMPTON – Rowan at John Lewis, West Quay Shopping Centre.
Mail order. Tel: 0238 021 6400.
WINCHESTER – C & H Fabrics, 8 High Street. Tel: 01962 843355.

HERTFORDSHIRE

BOREHAM WOOD – The Wool Shop, 29 Shenley Road. Mail order.

Tel: 0208 9052499.
HEMEL HEMPSTEAD – Needlecraft, 142 Cotteralls. Tel: 01442 245383.
ST ALBANS – Alison's Wool Shop, 63 Hatfield Road. Tel: 01727 833738.
WATFORD – Rowan at John Lewis, The Harlequin, High Street. Mail order. Tel: 01923 244266.
WELWYN GARDEN CITY – Rowan at John Lewis. Mail order.
Tel: 01707 323456.

ISLE OF MAN
PEEL – Fabric Centre, 2 Crown Street. Tel: 01624 844991.

KENT
BROADSTAIRS – The Wool Box, 66 High Street. Tel: 01843 86 7673.
CANTERBURY – Rowan at C & H Fabrics,
2 St George's Street. Tel: 01227 459760.
GREENHITHE – Rowan at John Lewis, Bluewater. Mail order. Tel: 01322 624123.
HEADCORN – Katie's Workbox, 15 High Street, Nr Ashford. Tel: 01622 891065.
E-mail: katies.headcorn@breathemail.net
MAIDSTONE – C & H Fabrics, 68 Week Street. Tel: 01622 762060.
TUNBRIDGE WELLS – Rowan at C & H Fabrics, 113/115 Mount Pleasant. Tel: 01892 522618.

LANCASHIRE
ACCRINGTON – Rowan at Sheila's Wool Shop, 284 Union Road, Oswaldtwistle.
Tel: 01254 875525.
E-mail: sheilaswoolshop@compuserve.com
BARNOLDSWICK – Rowan at Whichcrafts?,
29 Church Street. Mail order. Tel: 01282 851003. E-mail:
rowan@whichcrafts.co.uk Website:

www.whichcrafts.co.uk
LYTHAM – Rowan at Lytham Wools, Unit 7, Market Hall, Market Square. Tel: 01253 732150. Email:
Lythamwools@aol.com
Website: www.lythamwools.co.uk
PRESTON – Rowan at Bow Peep, 136 Liverpool Road, Longton. Mail order. Tel: 01772 614508.

LEICESTERSHIRE
HINCKLEY – Busy Fingers, 104 Castle Street. Tel: 01455 631033.
OAKHAM – The Wool Centre, 17 The Market Place. Mail order.
Tel: 01572 771358.

LINCOLNSHIRE
LINCOLN – Binns,
226/231 High Street. Tel: 01522 524333.

LONDON – CENTRAL
Rowan at Liberty, Regent Street, W1. Mail order. Tel: 020 7734 1234.
Rowan at John Lewis, Oxford Street, W1. Mail order. Tel: 020 7629 7711.
Rowan at Peter Jones, Sloane Square, SW1. Mail order. Tel: 020 7730 3434.

LONDON – WEST
CHISWICK – Creations, 29 Turnham Green Terrace, W4 1RS. Mail order. Tel: 020 8747 9697.
WEST EALING – Bunty's at Daniels, 96/122 Uxbridge Road, W13 9RA. Tel: 020 8567 8729. E-mail:
enquiries@bunty-wool.co.uk Website: www.bunty-wool.co.uk

LONDON – NORTH
Rowan at John Lewis, Brent Cross Shopping Centre, NW4. Mail order. Tel: 020 8202 6535.
FINSBURY PARK – Lenarow, 169 Blackstock Road. Tel: 020 7359 1274.
E-mail: michael@lenarow.co.uk

Website: www.lenarow.co.uk

LONDON – SOUTH
PENGE – Rowan at Maple Textiles, 188/190 Maple Road.
Tel: 020 8778 8049.
E-mail: mapletextiles@hotmail.com
BARNES – Creations, 79 Church Road, SW13. Mail order. Tel: 020 8563 2970.

MERSEYSIDE
LIVERPOOL – Rowan at John Lewis, Basnett Street. Mail order.
Tel: 0151 709 7070.
PRESCOT – Prescot Knitting Co Limited,
32 Eccleston Street. Tel: 0151 426 5264.
ST HELENS – The Knitting Centre, 9 Westfield Street. Tel: 01744 23993.
WALLASEY – Ryder House, 44 Seaview Road. Mail order. Tel: 0151 691 1037.

MIDDLESEX
SHEPPERTON – Arts & Yarns, Squires Garden Centre, Halliford Road.
Tel: 01932 781141.

NORFOLK
EAST DEREHAM – Central Norfolk Knitting Machines, 4 Aldiss Court.
Tel: 01362 694744.
NORWICH – Rowan at John Lewis, All Saints Green. Mail order.
Tel: 01603 660021.
SHERINGHAM – Creative Crafts, 47 Station Road. Tel: 01263 823153.
E-mail: info@creative-crafts.co.uk
Website: www.creative-crafts.co.uk

NORTHAMPTONSHIRE
HOLDENBY – Patchwork Palace, The Stable Yard, Holdenby Howe.
Tel: 01604 771303.
Website: www.patchworkpalace.com

NOTTINGHAMSHIRE
NOTTINGHAM – Rowan at John Lewis, Victoria Centre. Mail order.

Tel: 0115 9418282.

OXFORDSHIRE
BURFORD – Burford Needlecraft Shop, 117 High Street. Mail order. Tel: 01993 822136. E-mail:
rbx20@dial.pipex.com
Website: www.needlework.co.uk
OXFORD – Rowan at Rowan, 102 Gloucester Green. Mail order.
Tel: 01865 793366.

SOMERSET
TAUNTON – Hayes Wools, 150 East Reach. Mail order. Tel: 01823 284768.
YEOVIL – Enid's Wool & Craft Shop, Church Street. Tel: 01935 412421.

STAFFORDSHIRE
STAFFORD – Amerton Farm, Stowe by Chartley. Mail order. Tel: 01889 270294.
E-mail: amerfarm@aol.com
Website: www.amertonfarm.com
WOLSTANTON – K2 Tog,
111 High Street, Tel: 01782 862332.
E-mail: knit2tog@ntlworld.com

SUFFOLK
BURY ST EDMUNDS – Rowan at Jaycraft, 78 St John's Street.
Tel: 01284 752982.

SURREY
BANSTEAD – Maxime Wool & Craft Shop, 155 High Street.
Tel: 01737 352798.
CAMBERLEY – Army & Navy, 45–51 Park Street. Tel: 01276 63333.
GUILDFORD – Pandora,
196 High Street.
Tel: 01483 572558.
KINGSTON – Rowan at John Lewis, Wood Street. Mail order.
Tel: 020 8547 3000.

SUSSEX – EAST
BATTLE – Battle Wool Shop, 2 Mount

Street. Tel: 01424 775073.
BRIGHTON – Rowan at C & H
Fabrics, 179 Western Road.
Tel: 01273 321959.
EASTBOURNE – C & H Fabrics,
82/86 Terminus Road.
Tel: 01323 410503.
EAST HOATHLEY – The Wool Loft,
Upstairs at Clara's, 9 High Street.
Mail order. Tel: 01825 840339.
E-mail: Claras@netway.co.uk
FOREST ROW – Village Crafts,
The Square. Tel: 01342 823238.
E-mail: village.crafts@virginnet.co.uk
Website: www.village-crafts.co.uk
LEWES – Rowan at Kangaroo,
70 High Street. Mail order.
Tel: 01273 478554.
Website: www.kangaroo.uk.com

SUSSEX – WEST
ARUNDEL – Rowan at David's
Needle-Art, 37 Tarrant Street. Mail order.
Tel: 01903 882761. Fax: 01903 885822.
CHICHESTER – C & H Fabrics,
33/34 North Street. Tel: 01243 783300.
HORSHAM – Rowan at The Fabric
Shop, 62 Swan Walk. Tel: 01403 217945.
SHOREHAM BY SEA – Rowan at
Shoreham Knitting, 19 East Street.
Mail order.
Tel: 01273 461029. Fax: 01273 465407.
E-mail: sales@englishyarns.co.uk
Website: www.englishyarns.co.uk
WORTHING –
Rowan at The Fabric Shop,
55 Chapel Road. Mail order.
Tel: 01903 207389.

TEESIDE
HARTLEPOOL – Rowan at Bobby
Davison, 101 Park Road. Mail order.
Tel: 01429 861300.
E-mail: sales@woolsworldwide.com
Website: www.woolsworldwide.com

TYNE AND WEAR
NEWCASTLE UPON TYNE – Rowan
at John Lewis, Eldon Square. Mail order.
Tel: 0191 232 5000.

WARWICKSHIRE
WARWICK – Warwick Wools, 17 Market
Place. Tel: 01926 492853

WEST MIDLANDS
BIRMINGHAM – Rowan at Beatties,
16–28 Corporation Street. Mail order.
Tel: 0121 644 4000.
COVENTRY – Busy Fingers,
29 City Arcade. Tel: 02476 559644.
SOLIHULL – Stitches, 355 Warwick
Road, Olton. Tel: 0121 706 1048.
Rowan at John Lewis, Touchwood.
Mail order. Tel: 0121 704 1121.
WOLVERHAMPTON – Rowan at
Beatties, 71–78 Victoria Street.
Mail order. Tel: 01902 422311.

WILTSHIRE
CALNE – Handi Wools, 3 Oxford Road.
Tel: 01249 812081.

WORCESTERSHIRE
KIDDERMINSTER – Woolwise,
10 Lower Mill Street. Tel: 01562 820279.

NORTH YORKSHIRE
NR SKIPTON – Rowan at Embsay
Crafts, Embsay Mills, Embsay. Mail order.
Tel/Fax: 01756 700946.
E-mail: enquiries@embsaycrafts.com
Website: www.embsaycrafts.com
WHITBY – Rowan at Bobbins, Wesley
Hall, Church Street. Mail order.
Tel/Fax: 01947 600585.
E-mail: bobbins@globalnet.co.uk
Website: www.bobbins.co.uk
YORK – Rowan at Craft Basics,
9 Gillygate. Mail order.
Tel: 01904 652840.

SOUTH YORKSHIRE
BARNSLEY – Knit Wits, 11 Church
Street, Royston. Tel: 01226 725527.
SHEFFIELD – Rowan at John Lewis,
Barkers Pool. Mail order.
Tel: 0114 2768511.

WEST YORKSHIRE
CASTLEFORD – Bromley & Vairy, 5
Vickers Street. Tel: 01977 603069.
HEBDEN BRIDGE – Rowan at Attica,
2 Commercial Street. Mail order.
Tel: 01422 844327.
E-mail: info@attica-yarns.co.uk
Website: www.attica-yarns.co.uk
HOLMFIRTH – Rowan at Up Country,
78 Huddersfield Road. Mail order.
Tel/Fax: 01484 687803.
E-mail: info@upcountry.co.uk
Website: www.upcountry.co.uk
LEEDS – The Wool Shop, Whingate
Junction, Tong Road. Tel: 0113 263 8383.

THE WIRRAL
BRIMSTAGE – Rowan at Voirrey
Embroidery Centre, Brimstage Hall.
Tel: 0151 342 3514. Fax: 0151 342 5161.

WALES
ABERYSTWYTH – Clare's, 13 Great
Darkgate Street. Tel: 01970 617786.
CARDIFF – Rowan at David Morgan
Ltd, 26 The Hayes. Tel: 029 2022 1011.
CONWAY – Ar-y-Gweill, 8 Heol Yr
Orsaf, Llanrwst. Tel: 01492 641149.
FISHGUARD – Jane's of Fishguard,
14 High Street. Tel: 01348 874443.
PENARTH – David Morgan Ltd,
20 Windsor Road, Penarth, Cardiff.
Tel: 029 2070 4193.
SWANSEA – Rowan at Mrs Mac's,
2 Woodville Road, Mumbles.
Tel: 01792 369820.
WHITLAND – Rowan at Colourway,
Market Street. Mail order.

Tel: 01994 241333.
E-mail: shop@colourway.co.uk
Website: www.colourway.co.uk

SCOTLAND
ABERDEEN – John Lewis, George
Street. Mail order. Tel: 01224 625000.
ALFORD – Rowan at The Wool Shed,
Alford Heritage Centre, Mart Road.
Mail order. Tel: 01975 562906.
BERWICKSHIRE – Rowan at
Moondance Wools, Springhill Farm,
Coldingham, Eyemouth.
Tel/Fax: 018907 71541.
E-mail: moondancewools@aol.com

EDINBURGH
Rowan at John Lewis, St James Centre.
Mail order. Tel: 0131 556 9121.
Rowan at Jenners, 48 Princes Street.
Mail order. Tel: 0131 225 2442.
GLASGOW – Rowan at John Lewis,
Buchanan Galleries. Tel: 0141 353 6677.
ISLE OF ARRAN – Trareoch Craft
Shop, Balmichael Visitors Centre,
Shiskine.
Tel: 01770 860515.
KILMALCOLM – Strathclyde, Threads,
3 Drumpellier Place. Tel: 01505 873841.
LANARK – Strands, 8 Bloomgate.
Mail order. Tel: 01555 665757.
LINLITHGOW – Nifty Needles, 56
High Street. Tel: 01506 670435.
ST ANDREWS – Rowan at Di Gilpin
@ The Wool Merchants, Burghers Closer,
141 South Street. Tel: 01334 476193.
E-mail: di@handknitwear.com
Website: www.handknitwear.com
STIRLING – Rowan at McAree Bros
Ltd, 55–59 King Street. Mail order.
Tel: 01786 465646. Fax: 01786 464759.
Website: www.mcadirect.com

charts

RABBIT

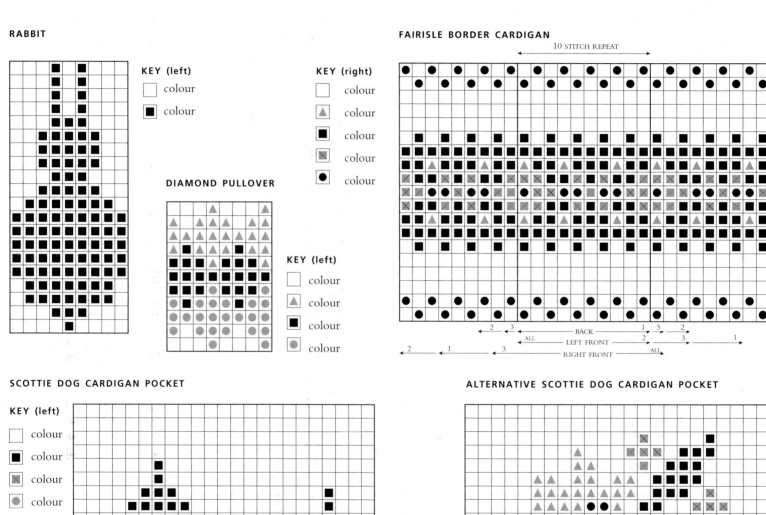

KEY (left)

□ colour

■ colour

DIAMOND PULLOVER

KEY (left)

□ colour

▲ colour

■ colour

● colour

KEY (right)

□ colour

▲ colour

■ colour

⊠ colour

● colour

FAIRISLE BORDER CARDIGAN

10 STITCH REPEAT

SCOTTIE DOG CARDIGAN POCKET

KEY (left)

□ colour

■ colour

⊠ colour

● colour

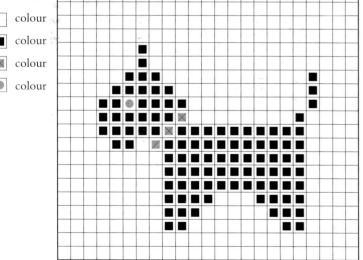

ALTERNATIVE SCOTTIE DOG CARDIGAN POCKET

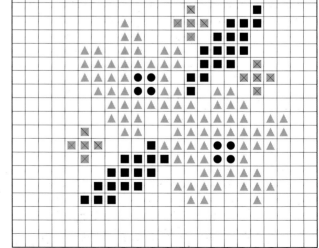

KEY (right)

□ colour

▲ colour

■ colour

⊠ colour

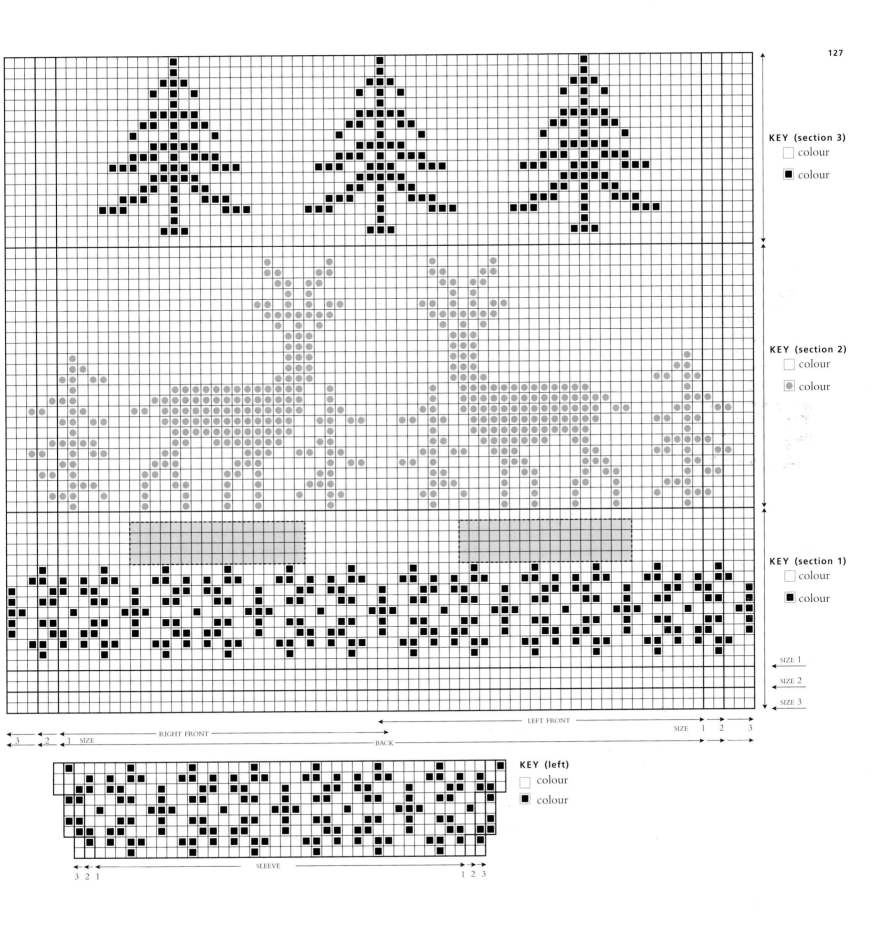

KEY (section 3)

☐ colour

■ colour

KEY (section 2)

☐ colour

◉ colour

KEY (section 1)

☐ colour

■ colour

SIZE 1

SIZE 2

SIZE 3

LEFT FRONT

SIZE   1   2   3

RIGHT FRONT

3   2   1   SIZE

BACK

KEY (left)

☐ colour

■ colour

SLEEVE

3 2 1   1 2 3

author's acknowledgements

My sincere and heartfelt thanks to the many people who have contributed to the creation of this book:

Kate Kirby and **Colin Ziegler** at **Collins & Brown** for their support. **Susan Berry** for her vision, commitment and endeavour. **John Heseltine** for his stunning photography, constant patience and professionalism. **Debbie Mole** for her superb design. **Eva Yates** for her pattern writing and checking skills, attention to detail and humour. **Sally Lee** for her eclectic making skills, tireless hard work and friendship. **Anne Wilson** for the chart design. **Stephen Sheard, Kate Buller and the team at Rowan and Jaeger** for their support and encouragement, and the wonderful yarns. **Kate and Lionel** at Cupcake, two of the nicest people with the nicest children's shop, for their unique clothes for styling. The lovely mums, **Bridget Turner, Serena Montgomery , Catrine Hayes** and **Donna Davis,**

And, of course, **Alice, Alex, Phoebe, George, Seth and Jacob** – inspiring, loving, mischievous and fun… **the perfect little cherubs!**